Enid Blyton

Mr Meddle's Bicycle

...and other stories

D0812663

B Bounty
Books

Published in 2014 by Bounty Books,
a division of Octopus Publishing Group Ltd,
Carmelite House
50 Victoria Embankment
London EC4Y 0DZ
www.octopusbooks.co.uk

An Hachette UK Company
www.hachette.co.uk
Enid Blyton ® Text copyright © 2014 Hodder & Stoughton Ltd.
Illustrations copyright © 2014 Octopus Publishing Group Ltd.
Layout copyright © 2014 Octopus Publishing Group Ltd.

Illustrated by Colin Wright.

ISBN: 978-0-75372-645-7

A CIP catalogue record for this book is available from the
British Library.

Printed and bound by CPI Group (UK) Ltd, Croydon, CR0 4YY

5 7 9 10 8 6

CONTENTS

Mr Meddle's
Bicycle

Mr Meddle had a bicycle of his own. It wasn't much of one, and it had no bell, and no pump. The bell had got broken and Mr Meddle had thrown it away. The pump had been lost.

"If only it had a saddlebag, I could put things in there," Mr Meddle thought. "But it hasn't even a saddlebag. It is most annoying."

The tyres were old and often got punctures. Mr Meddle hadn't enough money for new ones, so he had to keep mending the old ones and that annoyed him very much. "This bike is hardly worth keeping," he said to his friend, Mr Jinks. Mr Jinks looked at it.

"It doesn't look safe to ride," he said. "Meddle, why don't you get some work and, with the money you earn, buy yourself a new bicycle. Really you should. You'll have an accident on that one if you're not careful."

Well, Mr Meddle thought about what Mr Jinks said, and though he didn't like the idea of work, he did like the idea of a new bicycle. So when he heard that Mr Biscuit the baker wanted an errand boy, who could ride a bicycle, he decided that he had better get the job.

So off he rode the next morning on his old bike, propped it up against the window of the shop and went in to see Mr Biscuit.

"You don't look very bright to me," said Mr Biscuit, who knew a little about Mr Meddle and his ways. "Are you sure you could deliver my cakes and bread to the right addresses?"

"Of course," said Mr Meddle. "No doubt about that at all. And you should see me ride my bicycle! Top speed, tear-along, rush-about, get-out-of-the-way-there – my word, I'd soon deliver your goods for you."

"Hmmm," said the baker, doubtfully, "I'm not sure I want someone who rushes too much. He might spill the goods into the road."

"No, no," said Mr Meddle. "I'm a very careful fellow. I'd never spill a thing. You just try me, Mr Biscuit."

"Well, I will try you," said Mr Biscuit. "Now, do you see those bags over there? Well, the top one is for Lady Spend-A-Lot, and the second one is for Mrs Go-Along, and the third is for Mr Pay-Up. You take them this minute and come back here quickly."

"What will you pay me a week?" asked Mr Meddle. "You see, my bicycle is old and I want to buy a new one or else to get new tyres for it, and a new bell, pump and saddlebag. So I shall want good pay."

"We'll talk about good pay when I see if you do good work," said the baker. "Off you go."

Mr Meddle picked up the three bags carefully. He took them outside the shop. He put them into the basket on the front of the bicycle. Then he leaped on to the saddle and rode merrily off.

Mr Meddle didn't see that he had taken the wrong bicycle. He had taken Mr Biscuit's own bike, that had been left leaning against the shop window just in front of Mr Meddle's. Off he went on it, riding fast.

A dog ran across the road just in front of him. "Oh dear," said Mr Meddle, swerving to one side. "How I wish I had a good big bicycle bell! I'd give that dog the fright of its life!"

Now just as he said that Mr Meddle happened to look down at his bicycle

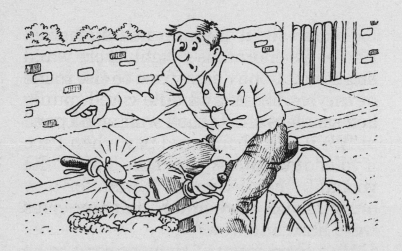

handles – and to his very great surprise he saw a nice large bicycle bell there. He almost fell off in astonishment.

"Look at that now!" he said, out loud. "I just wished I had a good big bicycle bell – and there it is! My word, this must be my wishing day, no doubt about that!"

He rang the bell – *jing-jing-jing-jing!* It made a wonderful noise. Meddle was very pleased indeed. "Now if only I had a nice black pump that would pump up my old tyres!" he said. "Shouldn't I feel glad then!"

He wondered if that wish had come true too. So he jumped off his bike and looked to see if a pump had appeared. And to his enormous delight, there was a bright black one neatly fixed to the frame of the bicycle. Mr Meddle could hardly believe his eyes. He took it off and looked at it.

"I'll just pump up my tyres," he thought. "No, I won't. I'll wish for new ones! I wish very much that my tyres were hard and new!"

He looked down at them as soon as he had wished – and lo and behold, there were new ones on the two wheels! It was simply amazing. Mr Meddle was filled with joy. He jumped on the bicycle and rode away merrily. He sang loudly as he went and when he met his friend Mr Gobo, Gobo stared at him in surprise.

"Why so merry?" asked Mr Gobo.

"Because it's my wishing day," said Mr Meddle. "Everything I wish for comes true. I wished for this bell, look – and the pump – and the new tyres. You know what an old bicycle mine was, wanting all new things. Well, isn't it marvellous now? As good as new?"

"How extraordinary!" cried Mr Gobo. "Wish for something else, Mr Meddle, and let me see it come."

Mr Meddle tried to think of something else he wanted. Ah, yes – a saddlebag. So he wished hard again. "I wish for a nice saddlebag, big enough to take quite a lot of things."

Both Mr Meddle and Mr Gobo looked at the back of the saddle to see if by any chance there was a saddlebag appearing – and, of course, there was one there. The two of them stared at it in delight. Really, this was marvellous.

"Wish for a new lamp," said Mr Gobo. So Mr Meddle wished for that too. But, alas, one didn't appear. Mr Biscuit's bike had no lamp, because it had a basket in front.

"The magic must be going," said Mr Meddle. "What a pity! Well, I must be off, Gobo. I've got these goods to deliver."

Mr Meddle delivered them safely – and then he stood and thought. Why should he bother to go back and do any more work for the baker, now that he had got all he wanted for his bicycle? That would be silly! So he rode home, popped his bike into the shed, and sat down to read the paper while the kettle boiled for a cup of tea.

Now Mr Biscuit waited and waited for Mr Meddle to come back, and he didn't. "Bother the fellow!" said Mr Biscuit, crossly. "There's all those other cakes to take out. I'll have to deliver them myself after all. I'll go on my bike."

He took the bags of cakes and went outside the shop to get his bicycle. But it wasn't there. Only Meddle's was there,

dirty and old, without a bell, pump or saddlebag, and with one tyre punctured. Mr Biscuit stared at it in horror.

"Where's my bike? Someone has taken it and left me his instead. Is it Meddle? The scamp, I half believe it is! I'll go and tell him what I think of him!"

He had to walk, because one of the tyres on Mr Meddle's bike was flat. But at last he arrived at Meddle's in a very bad temper. He hammered so loudly on the door that Mr Meddle fell out of his chair in fright.

"Meddle! Why didn't you come back?" yelled the baker.

Mr Meddle opened the door. "Oh, Mr Biscuit," he said, "I would have come back but some extraordinary things happened to me on the way here. It must be my wishing day, you see. I wished myself a bell – a pump – new tyres – and a saddlebag – and, do you know, they all appeared on my old bicycle. Wonderful, wasn't it?"

Mr Biscuit didn't believe a word of it. He glared at Mr Meddle, and said, "Where is your bicycle?"

"Out in the shed," said Mr Meddle. "I'll show you the things I wished."

He led the way out – but as soon as the baker set eyes on the bicycle he gave a shout of rage.

"I knew it! It's mine! You took mine and left me your own. Oh, you rascal! Oh, you rogue! I might have known you would do something like that. Now you come right back with me and fetch your bicycle and go out delivering the rest of the goods."

14

"But I tell you that's my bike!" said Mr Meddle, astonished. "Look, here's the bell I wished myself. I tell you, most extraordinary things happened to me this morning."

"And some more extraordinary things will happen to you if you don't come along with me at once," said Mr Biscuit, in such a terrible voice that Mr Meddle thought he had better do as he was told. So he walked back to the shop, while Mr Biscuit rode. And when he got there he saw his old bicycle leaning against the window, without any bell, pump, new tyres or saddlebag. Poor Mr Meddle! It did give him a shock!

"And now, away you go on your bike to deliver the rest of today's goods," said Mr Biscuit, fiercely. "Pump up your tyre with my pump – and put my pump back on my bike again – and then take the goods. And if you do anything silly I'll spank you with my biggest slipper!"

Poor Mr Meddle! He's working so hard now, but whether he'll ever make enough money to buy the things he wants I really don't know!

The
Foolish Frog

There was once a frog who was really very foolish. He thought he knew everything. When he was a tadpole he swam round telling everyone what nasty, leggy things frogs were – but even when he found that he was growing into a frog himself that didn't make him ashamed of his foolishness! No, he just went on being as boastful and as stupid as ever.

In the autumn, when the nights were frosty, the frogs began to think of going to sleep at the bottom of the pond, head downwards in the oozy mud. The toads hopped slowly out of the water and went to some damp stones they knew. They crept underneath, shut their bright, coppery eyes and went to sleep there. They would not wake up until the warm

17

springtime. But the foolish frog thought it was a waste of time to sleep through so many months. He didn't want to snooze under a stone. He didn't want to sleep in the mud at the bottom of the pond. No – he wanted to be up and about like the rabbits and the mice!

"It is a stupid idea to sleep so much of your lives away!" he said to the other frogs, when they told him it was time to prepare for the winter sleep. "Why should you be afraid of the winter? What does it matter if it is cold? I shan't mind!"

"You think you are so clever!" said the other frogs scornfully. "Very well – keep awake all the winter through if it pleases you! We shan't mind!"

So they left the foolish frog, swam down to the bed of the pond, tucked themselves into the mud and were soon sound asleep. They forgot the cold, they forgot the lack of flies and grubs – they slept peacefully and happily.

But the foolish frog still swam about in the pond. He wondered where the flies had gone that used to skim on the surface, and which tasted so good. He climbed out of the water and went to look for some in the ditch. But there were no flies, no caterpillars, no slugs to be found. The little frog felt very hungry.

He went back to the water and swam round sadly. Perhaps it would be a good idea after all to go to sleep. It wasn't much good being awake and hungry!

"Well, I'll go and have a nap in the mud," said the foolish frog at last. "But I shall not sleep all the winter through, as the others do. No – at the first possible moment, when the sun is warm, I shall wake up and enjoy myself again!"

He was soon asleep. He slept all through the month of December, and almost all through January. Then there came a warm spell. The sun shone on the pond and the frogs felt the warmth and stirred in their sleep. The foolish frog woke right up. Ah! How warm the water felt! Surely the winter was over!

He swam up to the surface. It was lovely in the sunshine. He swam down to the mud and woke up all the other frogs.

"Come!" he said. "The winter is over! The sun is shining. Wake up, and come and play."

But the oldest frog, after he had taken one look out of the water, swam back to the mud.

"Take no notice of the foolish one," he said. "Winter is not over. This is just a warm spell. It will be colder than ever soon. Bury your heads in the mud again, brothers and sisters, and go to sleep."

The frogs obeyed him – all but the foolish frog, who was very angry. He swam up to the surface by himself and enjoyed the warm sunshine – but, when

night came, and the sun went, something strange happened to the pond. The water became hard instead of soft, and icy cold. The pond was freezing! The water was turning into ice! The frog did not know what was happening and he was frightened. He swam round, but every minute it became more difficult.

The moon came out and shone on the freezing pond. It shone on the poor, foolish frog, now held tightly in the thickening ice. The frog opened his mouth and croaked mournfully.

A wandering hedgehog heard him and was surprised. A frog croaking at this time of year! How could that be? He peered about and saw the frog in the ice. He pattered across the hard pond and breathed down on the trapped frog.

"Friend, you are in a bad way," said the hedgehog. "You will be dead by morning unless I can help you. If I lie down by you I may melt the ice a little. Then you must struggle hard and kick out with your legs, and maybe you will get free of the ice."

The heat of the hedgehog's body thawed the ice a little and the frog found that he was able to move round. He

kicked out strongly with his legs and managed to get free. In a second he was hopping on the icy pond, and the hedgehog hurried away to the bank beside him.

"There is an old stone here in the ditch," said the kindly hedgehog. "Get under that and sleep for the rest of the winter, frog. You should not be awake now."

"Thank you," said the frog, humbly, for once really ashamed of himself, and very much frightened at his narrow escape.

He crept under the stone, shut his eyes and fell soundly asleep.

He was awakened by the croaking of the frogs in the pond. It was springtime now, and they had all awakened in excitement, glad to think the warm days had come again. They wondered where the foolish frog had gone.

"I expect he got frozen into the ice and is dead," said the oldest frog, scornfully. "He was foolish enough for anything!"

That made the foolish frog very angry.

He hopped out from under his stone and stared rudely at the old frog.

"No, I was not frozen into the ice," he croaked, untruthfully. "I had a very much finer winter than you did!"

"Oh, there is the foolish frog after all!" croaked all the other frogs in surprise. "Come into the pond and play, brother. Choose a nice little wife for yourself so that she may lay you eggs to grow into tadpoles!"

"I shall find a little pond where no other frogs are!" said the foolish frog. "My wife shall lay her eggs there, and we shall know that all the tadpoles in our little pond are ours! We shall teach them not to speak to or play with your tadpoles!"

With that he hopped off. Soon he met a pretty little green frog and asked her to be his wife. Then they went to find a nice little pond where she could lay her eggs.

The foolish frog found a large puddle left by the rain. "This will do nicely," he said to his green wife. "Come along!"

The little green frog laid many eggs in the puddle. The two frogs lived there contentedly, though all the toads and frogs that passed laughed at them scornfully.

The sun shone out warmly. The puddle grew smaller as the sun dried it. It grew smaller still. The little green frog became afraid and hopped off to the big pond. But the foolish frog stayed with the jelly-like eggs, hoping that they would soon hatch.

The puddle grew very small indeed – and then, alas, it dried up altogether! The mass of frog spawn dried up too, and the foolish frog was left in a hole by the side of the lane that led to the pond.

But still he would not move. He waited for the puddle to fill again. Soon, down the lane, there came the sound of clip-clopping hooves. The old farm horse was coming. She came nearer to the hole – nearer and nearer. One of her great hooves trod on the mass of dried frog spawn and another almost squashed the frightened frog to bits. He leaped out of the way and only his left hind foot was hurt.

Full of fear he hopped away to the pond and leaped into the cool water. His foot hurt him and he had lost his eggs – they would never hatch now. He was ashamed and miserable.

"Here is the foolish frog back again," croaked all the others. "Well, brother, did your eggs hatch into tadpoles in that puddle? Have you told them not to speak to our young ones?"

The foolish frog said nothing. He sank down to the mud and lay there, his foot aching.

"I am indeed foolish," he thought to

himself. "I thought I knew everything, but I know nothing. I will be humble in future and listen to what the others say."

Now he is no longer proud and foolish. He does what he is told. He listens to the older frogs. He is becoming wise and humble. Soon he will no longer be known as the foolish frog.

But you will always be able to tell him by his left hind foot. It got better but it grew crooked; so if you see a frog with a foot like that you will know that he once was the foolish little frog!

Santa Makes a Mistake

Have you ever heard the story of the night Santa Claus got stuck in the chimney? If you haven't, I really must tell it to you.

Not many years ago two children, Jane and George, lived with their Aunt Sarah and their Uncle Peter. Aunt Sarah looked after them very well, but as she didn't believe in fairies, or Santa Claus, she wasn't as nice as she might have been.

Jane and George believed in all those people, of course, and most of all in Santa Claus. They believed in him, because before their parents had gone away to India, Santa Claus had brought them presents each Christmas.

"All nonsense!" said Aunt Sarah crossly. "All nonsense! What would you

like me to give you for Christmas?"

"I'd like soldiers," said George.

"And I'd love a book of fairytales!" said Jane.

"Soldiers are silly toys," said Aunt Sarah, "and as for fairytales! Well! Just a pack of old nonsense! I shall give George a pair of nice warm gloves, and you a workbasket, Jane. It's time you learned to sew."

Now, George hated wearing gloves and Jane hated sewing. Still they were much too polite to say so, and just said, "Thank you very much, Aunt Sarah," and ran out to play.

"Let's write a note to Santa Claus,"

said Jane suddenly. "He always used to bring us what we asked for, George!"

"Yes, let's!" said George.

So the children sat down and wrote a letter. This is what they said:

Dear Santa Claus,

We hope you are well. Please do bring us a box of soldiers, and a book of fairytales, if you have some spare.

With love from Jane and George

"Now let's put it up the chimney," said Jane.

The two children ran up to their bedroom and poked the letter as far up the chimney as they could reach. They didn't say anything to Aunt Sarah about it, but just waited patiently for Christmas to come.

Now, I don't know whether you know it, but Santa Claus is rather fat, and he has to make himself very small in order to get down some of our narrow chimneys. He can do this easily by magic.

He travels with a small fairy who always peeps down the chimneys first to see whether his big master can get down without making himself smaller. Then, while Santa Claus goes down to fill the stockings, the fairy holds the reindeer steady.

Well, on Christmas Eve Santa Claus arrived on the roof of Aunt Sarah's house. The small fairy jumped down, and peeped into the chimney leading to Jane and George's room. It was nice big one. So Santa took his sack, stepped down from his sledge, and went up to the chimney pot. He swung his leg over it, and down he went.

But what do you think! He had made a mistake, and slipped down the wrong one! He had got into the chimney that led to the dining-room where Aunt Sarah was! And dear, oh dear! That chimney was terribly small! Santa Claus puffed and blew, and blew and puffed, and at last managed to squeeze himself down as far as the grate. Fortunately the fire had just gone out.

But Santa couldn't get out into the room! There he stuck, feeling very uncomfortable and very, very annoyed.

And, oh dear me! Aunt Sarah was dreadfully frightened. She was just going up to bed, when she suddenly heard a noise in the chimney, and saw two fat legs appearing above the big grate. She thought it was a burglar.

"Help! Help!" she cried. "It's a burglar!" and ran straight out of the room.

Uncle Peter had gone to bed and was fast asleep. Only Jane and George were awake, wondering if Santa Claus would come that night. When they heard Aunt Sarah calling, they jumped out of bed, and quickly rushed downstairs to help her.

No one was in the dining-room. Aunt Sarah was upstairs trying to wake Uncle Peter. Suddenly Jane pointed to the fireplace.

"Look, George! Look!" she said excitedly. "It's Santa Claus, but he's coming down the wrong chimney!"

Then a big voice came down the chimney and said, "Is that you, children? Give my legs a good pull and get me out of this chimney before your aunt comes back, will you?"

So the two children ran to the fireplace, caught hold of Santa Claus's big boots and pulled and pulled.

Then *slither-slither-crash*! Down came

Santa Claus and sat panting on the hearth-rug.

"Thank you! Thank you!" he said. "Quick! Show me your bedroom before anyone comes!" Jane and George took him up quickly just before Aunt Sarah and Uncle Peter came running down the passage.

"I made a mistake over the chimney," whispered Santa Claus. "Very silly of me! I'm much obliged to you for helping out. I've brought you your soldiers and fairy stories. But you can choose anything else you like for a Christmas present too, for being so kind to me. What would you like?"

"Can we choose anything in the world?"

"Yes, anything, but only be quick!" answered Santa Claus.

"Then, please, please, *please*, send us Mummy and Daddy home soon!" begged Jane and George together.

"All right, I will!" smiled Santa Claus. "Get into bed, I am going out of your chimney now. Goodbye!"

Aunt Sarah couldn't think where her burglar had gone, and Uncle Peter thought she must have dreamed him!

When Jane and George showed her their soldiers and fairytales next morning, she could hardly believe her eyes. They told her all about Santa Claus's visit and how he had come down the wrong chimney.

"Dear, dear, dear! You don't say so!" she said. "Well, if he does send your mummy and daddy back home soon, I will believe in him!"

And what do you think? The next day the childrens' parents suddenly walked up the garden path, just in time for the Christmas dinner! Did you ever hear of such a strange thing?

"Three cheers for Santa Claus!" said Jane and George. And I really think he deserved them, don't you?

Good Dog, Tinker!

Tinker belonged to Robin and Mary. Sometimes he could be very good but at others he could be very naughty. It didn't seem to matter which he was, though, the children loved him just the same.

One day Robin gave Tinker a juicy bone to gnaw. "It's good for your teeth," he said. "And you've been such a good dog lately I think you really do deserve a bone!"

"Miaow!" said Tabby the cat. She liked bones, too, though she could only scrape them with her rough tongue – she couldn't manage to chew them.

Tinker looked at her, with the bone in his mouth. He dropped it for a moment and spoke to her.

"You can miaow all day if you like,"

he said. "But you won't get so much as one single sniff at this bone."

"Wherever you bury it I shall find it," said Tabby. She was very clever at finding where Tinker buried his bones, and he didn't like it. It was too bad to bury a half-chewed bone, and then, when next he came to dig it up to find that it wasn't there because Tabby had found it.

"I shan't bury it this time," said Tinker. "I shall hide it where you will never be able to find it!"

He trotted off with the bone. He took it into the dark toolshed, and lay down to chew it. It was a very hard bone and

Tinker couldn't crunch it up. He had a lovely half-hour of chewing and gnawing. Then he heard Robin whistling for him.

"Walkie, walkie, Tinker!" called Robin, and Tinker knew he must put away his bone and go. But where should he put it? It must be somewhere clever, where Tabby would never find it. Tinker thought of all the garden beds in turn. No – Tabby would hunt in each one. Then he looked round the toolshed. Tabby never came in here! He would hide his bone somewhere in the toolshed.

He was lying on a sack. What about tucking it inside the sack? Then no one would see, and it would wait here for him to come back and chew it. That would be a fine hiding-place.

So Tinker pushed his lovely, smelly bone into the sack, and then scampered off to join Robin and Mary.

He forgot about his bone till the evening. Then he wanted it again. Off he went to the toolshed to have a good chew. But alas for poor Tinker, the door was shut fast! He stood and whined at it,

he scraped it with his paw. But it was no use, the door wouldn't open.

"Bad luck, Tinker!" said Tabby, nearby. "I suppose you've got your bone hidden in there! And you can't get at it. Dear, dear, what a pity to hide a bone in a silly place like that."

"Well, if I can't get it, you can't either," said Tinker with a growl, and ran off.

Now, the next day nobody went to open the toolshed to get out the tools. Poor old Tinker ran to the shed a dozen times that day, but he couldn't get in, and he couldn't manage to make Robin and Mary understand that he wanted to have the door opened.

So he had to go without his bone. Tabby sat and laughed at him, and when he ran at her in a rage she jumped up on to the bookcase and sat and laughed at him there. She really was a most annoying cat.

Now, that night somebody went to the toolshed. It was midnight and everyone in the house was fast asleep. The somebody was a robber. He had come to steal as many tools as he could out of the shed!

He was very quiet, so no one heard him, not even Tinker. He crept to the shed and found it locked. But he guessed that the key was not very far away, and he soon found it, hung on a nail just under the roof of the shed.

He opened the door and slipped inside. He switched on his torch and looked round at the tools. They were very good ones, and kept beautifully. The man grinned. Just what he wanted! He would be able to sell them for a lot of money. He took them down quickly from their nails and put them quietly together.

"I'd better slip them into a sack, in case anyone sees me on my way home," thought the robber. "I might meet the village policeman on his rounds." He looked about for a sack and saw one on the ground. It was the one which Tinker has pushed his bone into. The bone was still there, very, very smelly now. The robber picked up the sack and shook it. The bone slid to the bottom and stayed there.

The man quietly put all the tools into the sack, and then put the bundle over his shoulder. It was terribly heavy. The robber went out of the door, locked it, and hung up the key again.

He went softly to the bottom of the garden. He put down the sack and squeezed through the hedge, pulling the sack after him.

Then he put it on his shoulder again. He walked across the field with it, but it felt so heavy that he had to put it down on the ground again.

"I believe I could drag this sack across the field more easily than I could carry it," said the robber to himself. "It won't matter at all if it makes a bit of a noise now, because I am well away from any of the houses."

So he dragged the sack over the field.

He came to another hedge and squeezed through it. He went down a lane, still dragging the sack, and then, when he heard footsteps, he crouched down behind a bush, listening.

It was the village policeman. He had not seen or heard the thief, and he went slowly down the lane, thinking of the hot jug of cocoa that would be waiting for him when he got home.

The man crept out from his hiding-place and carried on down the lane. He came to the wood and slipped in among the dark trees. He made his way through the wood until he came to a big bank where he knew there were a lot of rabbit holes. He pushed the sack down a very big hole and pulled bracken and bramble sprays over the entrance.

"I'll come and get the tools when everyone has forgotten about them," he thought. Then off he went home.

Now, in the morning, Tinker ran to the toolshed early, for he knew the gardener would be there at eight o'clock to open the door. Sure enough, the man soon came along whistling. He took down the key and opened the door. Tinker darted in.

But the sack was gone! Tinker gave a howl of dismay – and at the same time the gardener gave a shout of surprise.

"Hey! What's happened to all the tools? They're gone!"

"Tools! Who cares about tools!" thought Tinker. "It's my bone that is really important. Oh, tails and whiskers, wherever can it be?"

The gardener went off to tell the children's father, and Tinker flew off to ask Tabby if she knew anything about his bone.

There was a great disturbance about the lost tools. The policeman was told and he came hurrying up to the house.

Nobody paid any attention at all to poor Tinker and his lost bone. Tabby laughed at him.

"You needn't laugh!" said Tinker. "It was an important bone, and the robber stole that as well as the tools. I do wish I knew where it was."

"Well, go and sniff about and see," said Tabby, beginning to wash herself.

Tinker thought that was a good idea. He ran to the toolshed. Yes – he could smell exactly where his bone had been, hidden in the sack in the corner. He ran out of the shed and began to sniff around the garden, hoping to get a smell of the bone somewhere.

When he came to the hedge at the bottom, he got very excited. There was the smell of bone there, quite distinctly.

That was where the robber had put down the sack to squeeze through the hedge. The sack smelled strongly of bone and the smell had been left on the ground beneath the hedge. Tinker had a very sharp nose and he could easily smell it.

He squeezed through the hedge. He ran into the field and sniffed about. He could smell nothing – till suddenly he came to the spot where the burglar had put his sack down and had begun to drag it instead. The smell of bone was very strong there. With his nose to the ground Tinker followed it across the field, to the second hedge, through the hedge and out into the lane.

"Fancy the robber taking my bone with him in the sack such a long way!" thought Tinker. "It must have seemed a very fine and important bone to him. Now – here we go again – down the lane – behind this bush – down the lane again – and into the wood. Off we go – through the trees – to this bank – and oh, *what* a strong smell of bone there is near this hole!"

Tinker scraped away at the rabbit-hole, sniffing his bone all the time. It was in the sack of tools, pushed down the hole. Tinker couldn't get it out.

"I'll go back and get Robin and Mary to help me," he thought. So he trotted back in excitement, and by pulling at Mary's skirt and Robin's trousers, he managed to make them understand that he wanted them to follow him.

In great astonishment they went down the garden, through the hedge, across the field, through the second hedge, into the lane, and then into the wood to the big rabbit-warren.

And there Tinker showed them the sack in the rabbit-hole. "My bone's in there," he woofed to them. "Get it out, please."

But Robin and Mary were not at all interested in the bone – they shouted with joy to see the tools in the sack!

"Daddy's tools! Look, they're all here! Let's take them home this very minute.

Won't Daddy be pleased? Oh, you very, very clever dog, Tinker, to find them for us!"

Tinker trotted home beside them, sniffing his bone eagerly. What a fuss there was when the children arrived home with all the tools!

They were emptied out and counted. Yes – they were all there! "Tinker, you shall have a very big, extra-juicy bone today, for being so clever!" said Robin.

Well – that was good news. Robin rushed off to get the bone from the butcher's, and Tinker put his head inside the empty sack and dragged out his beautiful old bone as well!

"I must say you were terribly clever to find all of the things that were stolen by the robber," said Tabby, in a very admiring sort of tone. Tinker was extremely proud.

"Well – I am rather a clever dog, you see," he said, "and as you seem to have learned that at last, I'll show you that I'm a very generous dog, too – you can have this bone, and I'll have the new one when it comes! And I say – have you heard? The policeman is going to hide in the wood till the robber comes to fetch the tools he hid. Then he'll be caught! I'm going to hide, too. I shall have fun!"

Tinker did enjoy his bone – and Tabby enjoyed the other one, too. Wasn't it a good thing Tinker hid his first bone in the sack?

A Story for Eastertime

There was once a chocolate shop in Fairyland, kept by old Mother Bootle. It was a most exciting shop. It had great big bottles full of sweets of all colours, wonderful boxes of chocolates, and candy, wrapped up in colourful paper.

But it was at Eastertime that the shop was most colourful of all, for then Mother Bootle had so many Easter eggs she didn't know what to do.

And such glorious ones they were! Chocolate ones, marzipan ones, ones that broke themselves in half when you said "Open, egg!" and showed you a surprise inside – perhaps a toy or a brooch. You can guess how all the fairies loved her shop.

One Easter her shop was more full of

eggs than ever before, and all day fairies, brownies, gnomes, and pixies looked longingly in at the window. They looked especially at one great big egg tied up with gold ribbon, right in the very middle of the window. It was a magic egg, and very expensive indeed.

Now Oll, the gnome, longed to buy that egg. So he counted out his gold, and he found he had twenty pieces. He tied them up in a bag and sat down to think.

"I don't believe that egg's more than twenty pieces of gold," he said. "But perhaps Mother Bootle wouldn't let me have it for that. The best thing to do would be to go into her shop when she is having lunch, leave the money on the counter and take the egg."

So you can see by that, that he was not a very nice gnome. He ran off to the shop. It was just lunch-time. He peeped inside. No one was there. Mother Bootle was having her lunch.

Quickly, Oll slipped inside, put his money-bag on the counter, caught up the magic egg, and ran! The egg was very heavy, for it was half as big as Oll himself.

He panted and puffed all the way home, and when he got there he put the egg down on his table and looked at it proudly.

"I'll untie the ribbon and say 'Open, egg'," he said, "and see what happens! I might find all sorts of wonderful things inside!"

He untied the gold ribbon. "Open, egg!" he cried in a loud voice.

Instantly the egg flew open, and out jumped a little imp! Oll looked just as scared as he could be. He never thought of anything like that at all.

"What can I do for you?" asked the imp, grinning. "I am your servant."

"Dear me, is that so?" said Oll, beginning to feel better. "Well, well! Let me see! You can sweep my bedroom for me!"

The imp took a broom, leaped upstairs, and began sweeping.

Oll heard him: *Swish! Swish! Swish!*

"Well, that's very nice," said Oll. "Now I've got a servant who will do all my work!"

He settled himself in a cosy chair and began to read.

Swish! Swish! Swish! went the broom upstairs. *Swish! Swish!*

"He's doing it very thoroughly!" said Oll after a time, "I'd better go and see if he's finished."

He ran upstairs, but oh, my goodness! That imp had swept the bedroom nearly bare! He had swept up the chairs and pictures, stools and books, and now he was beginning to sweep them out of the window.

"Stop!" cried Oll. "Stop! Whatever are you doing?"

"I can't stop working until you say the

56

proper words!" said the imp, sweeping a chair out of the window. "I'm magic!"

Well, Oll tried all the words he knew, but nothing he could think of stopped that imp.

"Perhaps you'd better tell me to do some other sort of work!" said the imp at last, when he had swept nearly everything out of the window or down the stairs. "I can do any work you like, you know!"

"Dear, dear, I wish I'd known that before," said Oll. "Go into the garden and wash all my dusters, then."

At once the imp ran downstairs, took a tub and water, and began to wash Oll's dirty dusters, while the gnome tried to put his bedroom straight.

Suddenly he heard shouts of laughter coming from the road outside, and looking out of the window, he saw a crowd of fairies and pixies leaning over his garden wall laughing.

It must be something that imp was doing! Oll rushed downstairs and out into the garden.

That imp had washed all the dusters and pegged them on the line, but he couldn't stop washing till he was told to

do something else. So what do you think he had done?

He rushed indoors and fetched the tables and chairs, and washed those! Then he hung them on the line, and you can't think how silly they all looked! It was no wonder everyone was laughing. He was just going to peg up a lot of saucepans when Oll rushed out.

"Stop! Stop!" he cried.

"I can't!" said the imp, grinning. "I'm magic! Think of something else for me to do!"

Well, would you believe it? Oll couldn't think of a single thing to tell the imp to do next! He just stood there, trying his hardest to think of something.

And then a dreadful thing happened.

The imp thought he would wash Oll next, and so he suddenly grabbed hold of him, put him in the tub and soaped him all over!

Splutter-splutter-splutter! went Oll, with soap in his mouth, eyes and nose. *Splish-splash!* "Help! Help! Fetch Mother Bootle!" he shouted.

One of the watching fairies flew off, laughing, to fetch Mother Bootle. Poor Oll had the water squeezed out of him, and then the wicked imp began to peg him on the line to dry!

And that's where Mother Bootle found him when she came hurrying down the road! She laughed till the tears ran down her cheeks to see Oll among all the chairs and saucepans!

"I took your magic egg!" wept Oll, "but

I'm sorry. Tell your imp to stop! I don't know how to make him!"

"Easy enough!" said Mother Bootle. "Go back to your egg!" she said to the imp.

Bang! Clap! He was gone, and through the open door Oll saw the split egg close together again. Mother Bootle unpegged him from the line.

"Well, you've been well punished for your dishonesty, Oll," she said. "You can have your gold back, unless you want to keep the egg. Do you?"

"No, no, no!" cried Oll. "Take the magic egg away. That imp has turned my house upside down, and made everyone laugh at me! Take the egg away!"

So Mother Bootle took the egg home, and left Oll to make his house tidy again. The egg was never seen in the window any more, and what happened to it nobody knows. But people do say it will turn up again one day.

I'm sure I don't want it, though. Do you?

The Land of
Golden Things

Once upon a time there was a king who
was very poor. He hadn't even a palace to
live in, and that made him very sad. He
had a crown to wear, it is true, but it
wasn't made of real gold, and it only had
eight precious stones in it.

He lived alone in a cottage with his
little daughter, Rosamunda. He had spent
all his money in going to war with
another country, and had lost the battle.
His people were too poor to help him – so
there he was, a king no better than a
pauper.

His cottage was built in a lovely place
looking out over the blue sea. He had
one cow that gave him creamy white
milk, four hens that laid him eggs every
day, and an old servant woman who

cooked nice, simple meals for him, grew fine vegetables in the little garden, and looked after Rosamunda.

The King was very unhappy. He longed for a palace, he longed for a treasure chest filled with gold, he longed for hundreds of servants, fine clothes and beautiful furniture. His little daughter grieved to see him so miserable, and tried to make him laugh and smile – but it was very difficult. Rosamunda was happy. She knew she was a princess, but she was glad she didn't live in a palace. She liked to feed the four hens, and milk

the gentle cow. She loved to paddle in the warm pools and walk out on the windy hills.

Best of all she liked to work in the little garden that belonged to the cottage. She loved to grow bright flowers and pick them for the jugs and bowls indoors. She used to take big bunches of sweet-smelling roses to her father, and make him look at how lovely they were.

"Look, Daddy," she would say. "Smell them. Aren't they beautiful?"

But the King wouldn't bother about them. If they had been made of silver or gold he would have seized them eagerly – but they weren't.

One day in the summertime he had a birthday. Rosamunda planned to give him a lovely present. She had a little rose-tree in a pot, one that she had grown all by herself, and she meant to give her father this.

She gave him a birthday hug, and then suddenly brought out the dear little tree. It was covered with tiny pink buds and blossoms, and was just like a fairytale

tree. Rosamunda felt sure her father would love it.

But, do you know, he didn't even look at it properly! He just glanced at it, and said "Thank you, my dear," and nothing else at all. He didn't say, "Oh, what a lovely little tree! How I shall love to have it and look after it!" Rosamunda was dreadfully disappointed.

"Daddy, darling, you must be sure to water it every single morning before the sun gets hot," she said to him. "It is rather a delicate little tree, so please see that it gets enough to drink."

The King put it on the windowsill in his tiny bedroom, and then forgot all about it. He sat down and thought of the birthday he would have had if he had been a king with lots of money and a rich kingdom.

"I should have had a hundred guns fired off," he thought. "Then people would have come to my throne bringing gorgeous presents. At night I would have given a grand party, and had kings and queens, princes and nobles for my guests. Wouldn't it have been fine!"

He made himself so miserable, grieving over this, that for quite a week he forgot to smile at Rosamunda. She was sad because she loved him. She felt sure, too, that he had forgotten to water the little tree she had given him.

One bright morning the King went for a walk through the fields that lay behind his cottage. As he went on his way, a stranger approached him. He was a fine looking youth, tall and strong.

"Can I help you?" asked the King, seeing that the stranger seemed to have lost his way.

"That would be kind of you," said the youth. "I want to get back to the place where I have left my carriage, and I cannot find the way. It was by a lovely little blue stream that ran through a wood."

"You have wandered for miles then," said the King. "I know the stream. Let me take you back myself. I am sorry I have no servant to guide you, but there is only the old woman in the cottage. I am a king, but have none of the things a king should have, as you can see – except for my crown."

"That is very good of you," said the stranger. So he and the King walked over the fields together, and after about two hours came to where the carriage had been left.

How the King stared when he saw it! It was made of pure gold, and shone in the sun so brightly that the King was dazzled when he looked at it.

There was a coachman there, clad in a golden livery, and eight footmen, all in gold breeches and coats of fine brocade.

"How rich you must be!" the King said enviously.

"Let me drive you to my kingdom, and you shall see it," said the strange youth. "It is supposed to be one of the most wonderful places in the world."

The King stepped into the carriage. The coachman flicked his golden whip, and the horses started forward. How fast they went! The King knew they must have some sort of magic in their blood for they went too fast for him to see anything out of the windows at all. Trees, houses and hedges flashed by in a long line.

At last the carriage stopped in front of a vast, golden palace. The King shut his eyes after giving it one glance for it was so dazzling. He went up the golden steps, feeling quite dazed.

The stranger gave him a wonderful meal served on golden plates with an edging of diamonds. He drank from a golden goblet studded with red rubies and green emeralds. Servants clad in rich golden draperies stood in dozens around the golden hall. How the King envied all this richness!

"If only I had a little of your marvellous store of gold," he said to the stranger, "how happy I should be!"

"You shall have as much as my carriage will hold when it takes you home again," said the youth. "I have so much that I am glad to get rid of some of it."

After the meal the King went to see the treasure-house. There were not only bags of gold there, and chests filled to the brim with golden bars, but also rare treasures. There was a golden apple that could make anyone who was ill feel better at once merely by holding it in his hand. There was a goblet set with sapphires which was always full of the rarest wine in the world, no matter how much was drunk from it.

The King looked at all these things longingly. Then he saw a beautiful mirror, and he picked it up to look at it.

"That mirror will show you the picture of anyone you think of," said the stranger. "Think of someone now, and take a look in the mirror."

The King at once thought of one of his generals, and looked into the mirror. A picture came there, and he saw an old bent man working in a potato field. When the man stood up, the King saw that it was his old general.

"Dear, dear!" he said, sadly. "To think that my famous old general should be working in a potato field!"

Then he thought of the king who had defeated him, and immediately a new picture came into the mirror. It showed a fat, ugly man sitting at a well-laden table. He wore a heavy crown, and he frowned at his queen, who was sitting beside him. She was speaking sharply to him, and though the King could not hear what was being said, he knew that she was cross with his old enemy and was scolding him.

"Aha!" he said. "So my foe has grown fat, and his queen leads a miserable life!"

Then he turned to the youth. "This is a marvellous mirror," he said. "May I have it, for it would pass away many a weary hour for me?"

"What will you give me for it?" asked the youth. "It is a very valuable thing."

"I have so little that I can give," said the King. "Would you like a cow? Or a hen, perhaps?"

The youth laughed. "No," he said. "You shall give me whatever you see first tomorrow morning! As soon as you set eyes on it, it will vanish away to my kingdom. It will be amusing to see what comes!"

The King took away the mirror happily. He saw many bags of gold stowed away in the carriage that was to take him back to his cottage, and on the way home he made all kinds of plans.

"I shall build myself a fine house," he decided, "and get a new crown. Rosamunda shall have her first silken dress and a golden necklace."

It was late when he arrived back at the cottage. The footman helped to dump all the bags of gold under the tree in the little garden, and then off went the golden carriage into the night.

The King was tired. He undressed and got into bed, thinking of the wonderful mirror.

"I shall look at the little rose-tree that Rosamunda gave me for my birthday," he thought. "That shall be the very first thing I set eyes on. It is about the only nice thing in this bedroom. I am sure the stranger will be pleased to see it arriving in his kingdom."

He fell asleep. When the early morning sun streamed into his room, he still slept.

But Rosamunda was awake. She was out in the garden singing merrily. She looked up at her father's bedroom, and wondered if he was awake. She caught sight of the little rose-tree on his window-sill, and she saw that it was drooping.

"Poor little tree, it wants water," she said. "I will creep into Daddy's room and water it before the sun gets hot."

She took a jug, filled it with water, and went up to her father's room. She knocked, and then knocked again. When she got no answer, she opened the door, and peeped in. She saw the King lying fast asleep in bed, so she ran lightly across the floor to the window, and began to water the rose-tree.

At that moment the King awoke. He remembered that he meant to look at the tree first of all, so he opened his eyes and glanced across at the window where the tree stood.

But Rosamunda stood there in front of it, watering it! The King saw her immediately – and then she vanished before his eyes!

"Oh!" said the King, in horror. He sat up, and rubbed his eyes. Then he looked again. There stood the little tree, and there on the floor lay the jug that his little daughter had been using. But Rosamunda was quite gone.

"She's vanished to the land of golden things!" groaned the King. "Oh, what shall I do?"

He got up and went to the window. Then he saw all the bags of gold lying under the tree in the garden, and in delight he rubbed his hands and laughed. He forgot all about Rosamunda, and dressed quickly in order to go and run his hands through the golden coins.

He thought no more of his little girl all that day till the old servant came to him in distress and said that she could not find Rosamunda anywhere.

Then the King remembered what had happened, and told the servant about it.

"Oh, oh, oh!" she sobbed, wringing her hands. "To think of my little pet all alone in a strange land! Oh, you wicked man, to forget all about your little lamb like this! What is gold compared with Rosamunda's silken hair, merry eyes, and loving smile?"

The King suddenly felt miserable. How could he have forgotten his happy little daughter? He went red with shame, and turned away his head. But how could he get Rosamunda back? He did not know the way to the land of golden things.

All that week the King missed his little daughter badly. He could remember Rosamunda's sweet smile and her loving voice. He could remember the feel of her warm hugs and kisses. He longed to hear the patter of her little feet. But instead of Rosamunda in the garden, he had bags and bags of gold.

Then he remembered the wonderful mirror he had brought back with him, and he looked into it. He thought of Rosamunda, and immediately the mirror showed him a picture of her.

She was standing in a garden, picking roses from a glittering bush. But alas for Rosamunda! The roses were golden, and

had no smell, no softness, no beauty.

The King watched his little daughter in the mirror. He saw big tears streaming down her cheek as she held the hard rose in her hand. He knew how much she must miss her own little cottage garden, with its pretty, sweet-smelling flowers growing everywhere from seeds she herself had planted.

"Oh, if only I could get my little daughter back again, I would be happy here for the rest of my days!" he said. "I would willingly give back this gold and this marvellous mirror if I could have Rosamunda in their place! I have been a foolish man, always pining for riches when beside me I had Rosamunda, worth more than a hundred thousand bags of gold. How hard she tried to please me, how sweet she was, and how she loved me!"

The unhappy King walked out into the fields and wept loudly. Suddenly he saw the bright stranger again and he ran up to him eagerly.

"Tell me about Rosamunda!" he cried. "Is she wanting me? Is she sad?"

"Very sad," said the stranger gravely. "Will you take her back, in exchange for the gold and the mirror, O King?"

"Willingly, willingly!" cried the King with joy. "I am cured of my foolishness. I no longer wish for anything more than my little daughter. If I have her I am richer than any king in the whole world!"

"She is in my carriage over there," said the stranger, with a smile.

The King turned and saw the golden carriage standing in a narrow lane nearby. He scrambled through the hedge, tearing his clothes terribly, but he did not care one bit! There was Rosamunda looking out of the carriage. When she saw her father she gave a shriek of

delight, opened the door, and fell into his arms. How they hugged and kissed one another! How they laughed and cried! They quite forgot about the stranger.

By the time they remembered him, he was gone. Vanished too were the bags of gold, the mirror, and the wonderful golden carriage. But the King laughed to see them gone. He had Rosamunda back, and that was all he cared about.

"Daddy, you seem different," said Rosamunda. "I believe you love me after all. We will be happy together now, won't we?"

"We will!" said the King. "You and I will work in the garden together, and go for walks together, and row on the sea together. Won't we be happy, Rosamunda?"

"Throw your crown away, Daddy!" cried the little girl. "Don't be a silly old king with no money and lots of frowns and sighs. Be a nice daddy, and smile and laugh every day!"

She took the crown from the King's head and threw it into a nettle-bed! The King looked horrified at first – but soon he laughed. And never again did he want to be rich, for he knew that was foolishness. Now he and Rosamunda are as happy as the day is long.

As for the little rose-tree she gave him for his birthday, they planted it out in the garden. It has climbed all over the cottage now, and if you happen to visit them in the summertime, you will see how lovely it is.

A Knot in
His Tail

The clockwork mouse was always very busy. He ran here and there, he sniffed under the mats and he poked his sharp little nose down every hole he could find.

Sometimes he hid a crumb under the end of the hearth-rug.

"Now that fat old teddy bear won't find it!" he said to himself. "I'll remember to come and get it tomorrow."

But he had such a bad memory that he never remembered where he put anything. Teddy would often find the crumb before he did, and that really did make Mouse most awfully cross.

"I wish I could remember better," he said to his friend, the little doll. "I do really. How can I remember things, Lotty?"

"Well," said Lotty, "when I want to remember something I always tie a little knot in a corner of my hanky – like this, – and then when I see the knot, I say to myself, 'Ah, I put that knot there to remind me to do this or that.' And that's how I always remember."

"That's a very good idea," said the clockwork mouse. "It really is. I'll do it myself. Oh, bother! I can't!"

"Why can't you?" asked the little doll.

"Because I haven't got a hanky," said Mouse. "You can't tie knots in a hanky if you haven't got one."

"I'll lend you one and you can keep it in your pocket," said Lotty.

"No, I can't," said Mouse. "I haven't got a pocket. I've often felt all over me for one, but I know I haven't got one."

"Well, then, I really don't know what you can do!" said Lotty. "Oh, wait a minute – yes, I do!"

"What can I do?" said Mouse, excited.

"You can tie a knot in your tail!" said the little doll. "Then, when you see the knot, it will remind you that you must remember something."

"That's a very good idea!" said Mouse. "I want to remember where I put a tiny bit of chocolate, Lotty. I put it down the hole that is by the fireplace. I'm going to eat it when I feel hungry."

"Well, tie a knot in your tail, then, and you will remember about the chocolate whenever you see the knot," said Lotty.

So the clockwork mouse tied a beautiful knot in his long tail. Then, before he and Lotty could talk any more, Jane, the little girl whose toys they were, came into the playroom and picked up Lotty.

"You're coming for a ride in my toy

pram," she said. "I'm taking you to play next door. Come along, Lotty!"

Now, it was a funny thing, but Mouse didn't notice the knot in his tail at all. He really wasn't used to looking at his tail. He took no notice of it, unless somebody happened to tread on it, then he squealed. So he didn't see the knot again, and he forgot all about it. Lotty had been lent to the little girl next door, and didn't come back – so she couldn't remind him about it, either.

It was Teddy who told him about it. "Mouse!" he cried. "Somebody has played a trick on you!"

"Whatever do you mean?" asked Mouse.

"Well, look at your tail!" said Teddy. "Someone has crept up behind you when you were asleep, and tied your tail into a knot! Ho ho ho!"

The mouse looked at his tail. He felt very cross indeed to think that anyone should dare to creep up behind him and do such a thing. He glared round at the toys.

"Who's done this unkind thing? I shall bite the one who did it! My tail hurts dreadfully with a knot in it!"

That wasn't true. It didn't hurt a bit. But Mouse loved to make a fuss. He tried to undo the knot, but he couldn't. It was really tied very tight indeed.

"Oh, it's too bad!" he wept. "I can't undo it! It's hurting me. Whatever shall I do, whatever shall I do?"

"I'll undo it," said Teddy, with a giggle. But he was very rough with his big paws,

and the mouse squealed so loudly that Angela, the biggest doll, made the bear stop trying to undo the knot.

Mouse made quite a puddle on the floor with his tears. Angela felt sorry for him.

"It's a shame, Mouse," she said. "It really is. People oughtn't to tie knots in someone else's tail. Whoever did it ought to be punished."

"Can I bite the horrid person hard?" asked Mouse, a large tear dripping off the end of his whiskers.

"That would not be a nice thing to do, Mouse," said Angela. "Let's find out who it was and we'll punish them fairly. Somebody here must have done it. Now, I think we are all truthful toys. I'll ask everyone, and whoever did it, even if it was for a joke, must own up. I'm sure no one is too cowardly to own up."

"I'm certain that nasty Teddy did it," wept Mouse.

"I didn't do it, so there!" said Teddy crossly. "I might have, if I'd thought of it – but I just didn't think of it – and if I had I'd have put at least twelve knots into your silly tail, not one! Ho ho ho!"

"You're horrid," said Mouse. "If you'd got a tail at all, which you haven't, I'd nibble the end right off!"

"Don't talk like that," said Angela, shocked. "It sounds most unkind. Now, you didn't do it, Teddy. Was it you, Sailor Doll?"

"No, of course not," said the sailor doll at once.

"Did you, Yellow Dog?" asked Angela, turning to the dirty old yellow dog who

had lived in the playroom almost longer than any of them. He shook his old head.

"No, I didn't," he said. "I'm too old to play tricks like that."

Angela asked every toy in the playroom, and they all said no, they hadn't tied the knot in Mouse's tail. It was very puzzling.

"Somebody's not telling the truth!" said Mouse, fiercely. "And that's even worse than tying a knot in my tail. I think I'm going to bite the person very hard when we find out who it is, even if it isn't very nice of me."

"We'll see about that," said Angela. "We can't do anything until we find out who it is. Wait a bit, though – Lotty isn't here. Maybe it's Lotty! We'll ask her when she comes back."

Lotty came back that evening. The toys crowded round her to hear her news. It wasn't often that any of them went away to stay.

Then Angela asked her about the knot in Mouse's tail. "We're all rather worried," she said, "because some cruel toy has tied a knot in the clockwork mouse's tail, and we don't know who. We can't undo the knot, and it hurts poor Mouse terribly. I do hope it isn't you, Lotty, because we always thought you were Mouse's friend."

"So I am," said Lotty, and she laughed suddenly. "No, I didn't tie the knot. But I know who did! Ho ho ho!"

"Ah! You know who did?" cried Mouse, and he looked very fierce. "Tell me, then, and I'll bite him hard!"

"You tied it yourself, Mouse!" said Lotty, and she laughed again. "Ho ho ho! – what a memory you've got!"

"Tied a knot in my own tail!" cried

Mouse, scornfully. "Why should I do such a silly thing?"

"It wasn't such a silly thing," said Lotty. "Don't you remember saying you wished you had a hanky so that you could tie a knot in it to remind you that you had hidden a bit of chocolate down the hole by the fireplace? And I said, 'Well, tie a knot in your tail instead,' – and you did!"

The toys all stared at the clockwork mouse. He went red to the tip of his nose.

"Oh," he said. "Yes. I do remember now. Oh, dear me!"

"Ho ho ho!" roared Teddy. "He did it himself. Mouse, go and bite yourself very, very hard for being so naughty as to put a knot in your own tail. Ho ho ho!"

"You've been rather silly, haven't you?" said Angela, and Mouse ran away and hid in a dark corner. He looked at his tail. He undid the knot quite easily with his teeth. Then he remembered the bit of chocolate that the knot was supposed to remind him about. He ran to the hole where he had hidden it away.

But it had gone! Teddy had been to find it, and had eaten it up. He had a tiny smear of chocolate on his nose. He saw Mouse looking for it and laughed.

"I don't need a knot in my tail to help my memory!" he said. "I'm not so silly as you are, Mouse!"

The
Wind's Party

"I want to blow hard!" said the autumn wind. "I want to rush round and sweep things away in front of me. I haven't had a good blow for ages."

"Well, blow then," said a little cloud. "I think I shall rather like it if you do!"

"I don't want to waste all my breath on a little thing like you!" said the wind. "I want to blow hundreds and thousands of things away. I want to have some real fun."

"Well, have a party, and ask the trees to come to it!" said the little cloud. "Tell them to put on party dresses of all colours – and then blow as hard as you can! You'll have such fun blowing off their red, yellow, orange and brown leaves!"

"That's a good idea!" said the wind. "I could blow the leaves high in the air, and all round about – and then I could puff them along the ground, and sweep them into the ditches. I think I could really have some fun doing that."

So the wind went round about whispering in among all the trees. "Come to a party, all of you! Come to a party! Put on your prettiest colours, and come to the wind's party!"

The beech put on a dress of brightest gold, and shimmered in the sunshine. The hazel put on pale gold and so did the silver birch.

The chestnut put on orange and yellow, and the wild cherry put on the brightest pink. The oak turned a russet brown, and the creeper on the houses nearby flamed into crimson.

"Fine, fine!" cried the wind, as he swept around. "Are you ready for the party! It's a party for your leaves, you know. I want them to play with, I want to make them dance and twist in the air. Are you ready?"

Then, with a rush, the wind swept through the trees. The frost had touched them the night before, and they were loose. The wind pulled them off.

Then off into the air went the coloured leaves, red, yellow, pink and brown, whirling and twirling, swaying and falling.

What a game the wind had with them! How he blew them about, and made them dance and prance! Soon the trees were bare, for their coloured party frocks were gone!

"Come and play too!" cried the autumn wind to the children. "Come along, come along! For every leaf you catch before it reaches the ground you shall have a happy day next year!"

Let's go and catch them as they whirl in the air. Let's see if we can catch three hundred and sixty-five, a whole year of wonderful, happy days!

We're coming to your party too, autumn wind. Please wait for us, do!

The Little Girl
Who Didn't Think

Once upon a time there was a little girl
who didn't think. Her name was Mollie,
and her mother was at her wits' end to
know how to make her think. Her father
was very upset about it, too, but he
couldn't do anything either.

Mollie did all sorts of silly things
because she didn't think. She nearly
always put her shoes on the wrong feet,
and twice she came down to breakfast
in her petticoat because she had
forgotten to put her dress on. And once
she even went to school on a Saturday,
because she had forgotten that the school
shut for the weekend. She was most
surprised to find that no one was there.

Now, one day a new baby came to
Mollie's house. He was the dearest,

tiniest, loveliest thing, and he belonged to Mollie's mother and father.

Mollie loved him and loved him and loved him. She loved to hold him and sing to him. And the baby loved Mollie and smiled at her, and held her little finger in his funny little hand. Father was very pleased to see how fond Mollie was of the baby. He thought perhaps it would make her more careful in all sorts of ways. But it didn't seem to, for the very day after he had thought that, Mollie was silly enough to shake pepper on her porridge instead of sugar! And that meant her porridge was all wasted, of course.

The baby grew big and bonny – but then one day he fell ill. He lay in his crib and coughed and the doctor came to see him every day.

"Will Baby get better?" Mollie kept asking. "Will Baby get better? Oh, please, please, make him better, Doctor!"

"He'll get better all right," said the doctor, smiling. "Don't you worry your little head! Help your mummy all you

possibly can by being a really good and
thoughtful little girl."

But Mollie didn't help her mother
much. That very same evening she went
to bed in all her clothes, because she had
forgotten to get undressed. Did you ever
hear such a silly thing?

One afternoon Mother, Baby and
Mollie were all together. Baby was lying
on Mother's lap fast asleep and she was
very pleased.

"If only he doesn't have another bad coughing fit!" said Mother. "But I don't think he will! Wake up, Mollie! You look as though you are half asleep! Go and fetch me the blue bottle you will see on the table downstairs in the dining-room. Then, if Baby does have a bad turn, I'll give him some of his new medicine."

Mollie didn't stir.

"Bless the child!" said Mother. "Dreaming as usual! Mollie! Go and get me the blue bottle on the dining-room table!"

"The blue bottle on the dining-room table," said Mollie, dreamily. "Yes, Mummy."

She jumped up and went downstairs.

"Blue bottle," she said, "blue bottle. I mustn't forget."

She went into the dining-room. On the table crawled a large bluebottle fly.

"Ah! There's the bluebottle!" said Mollie. "What a funny thing for Mummy to want. I must try to catch him."

But the bluebottle didn't want to be caught at all. With a loud buzz he flew off the table and banged straight into the windowpane. There he buzzed up and down angrily.

Mollie stood on a chair and tried to catch him. Off he flew again all round the room and came to rest on a picture. Buzz! Mollie just missed him again and he flew off.

Round and round the room they went,

Mollie trying her very hardest to catch the bluebottle, but she couldn't, he was far too quick.

Upstairs, Mother was wondering what in the world Mollie was doing. And suddenly Baby woke up and began to cough badly.

"Mollie! Mollie! Bring that blue bottle!" cried her mother anxiously.

Mollie heard her and scurried round faster and faster than ever after the buzzing bluebottle.

Upstairs, Baby's cough started getting worse.

"Mollie! Be quick!" cried Mother. "Baby's not well!"

Mother couldn't think why Mollie didn't come and she dared not wait any longer for Baby's medicine, so downstairs she went, holding Baby as gently as she could in her arms.

At the door she was met by Mollie, holding something tightly in one of her hands.

"I've got it, Mummy, I've got it!" she panted. "But it took me ever such a

long time before I could catch it!"

"Catch it!" said Mummy. "Catch what? Whoever heard of any one catching medicine? Did the bottle walk right off the table and start to run round the room? Silly child! Look, there's the blue bottle of medicine I told you to get for Baby, lying in the middle of the table!"

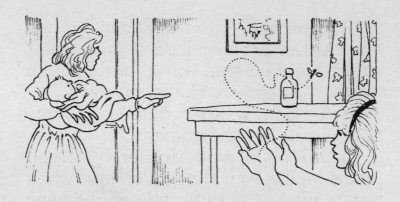

Mollie stared at the medicine bottle.

"Oh!" she said, "I thought you meant this bluebottle fly I've caught," and she showed her mother the little fly which she was holding in her hand.

"Ugh! The nasty thing! Throw it away and go and wash your hands at once!" said Mother, giving Baby his medicine. "You might have known I wouldn't have wanted anything like that for Baby, and if only you had listened to me and thought for a minute, you wouldn't have been so silly!"

"Oh dear! And I spent such a long time running round the room trying to catch that bluebottle," Mollie said. "I am a silly-billy, aren't I, Mummy?"

"You certainly are," said her mother. "You are a real silly-billy. But you needn't be because you can think hard enough when you want to, Mollie, my dear!"

Mollie went very red. "Please, is Baby all right now?" she asked.

"I think so," said Mother, "but you know, Mollie, your thoughtlessness when you went to get the bottle might have been very serious for him and made him much worse. Go and wash your hands now."

Mollie went – and as she washed her hands she made her mind up to never be so silly again, just in case she might go and hurt someone else by not thinking.

And what do you think Mother called her whenever she thought Mollie wasn't thinking enough? Miss Bluebottle!

The
Vanishing Nuts

In the garden belonging to Apple Tree Cottage there were twenty-two nut-trees. Susan, George and Peter's great-grandfather had planted them, because he had been very fond of nuts – and now they had grown into fine trees that bore heaps of big nuts every year.

Susan, George and Peter were very fond of nuts too. They helped to pick them and in return they were given a big dishful for themselves. They helped to pack up boxes of nuts too, to send away to their father's brother and sisters. Nut-time was a very busy time indeed!

Father always used to put aside a boxful of the very finest nuts for Christmas time. He carried it up into the attic room, and popped it on the floor

108

there. Then, at Christmas, the box was taken downstairs and the nuts were set out in pretty little dishes.

One autumn the nut-trees grew the biggest nuts they had had for years. Father was very pleased. He chose some fine ones to store away for Christmas, and George helped him to carry the box upstairs to the attic.

"Now, none of you children are to go to the attic for nuts," said Father. "But you all know that, very well, don't you?"

"Yes, Daddy," said Susan, George and Peter. "We promise we won't."

Father didn't think any more about the Christmas nuts until one day when he happened to go upstairs to fetch a pair of old boots from the attic. He happened to glance at the box of nuts – and then he stood still and frowned.

"Someone's been taking those nuts," he said. "Now, whoever can it be?" He went downstairs and found Mother.

"Have you taken any of the Christmas nuts from the attic?" he asked.

"No, dear," said Mother in surprise. "Why?"

"Because quite a number have gone," said Father, frowning. "Is it the children, do you think?"

"Oh, I hope not," said Mother, looking worried. "I don't think they'd take anything without asking. Do you?"

"Call them in here and I'll ask them," said Father. So Mother called all the children, who were out in the garden, and the three of them soon came in and trooped into their father's study.

"Have any of you been taking the nuts from the attic?" said Father. "Have you, Susan?"

"Oh, no," said Susan. "Of course not, Father."

"What about you, George?" asked Father.

"I haven't either," said George.

"Have you, Peter?" said Father.

"No, I haven't," answered Peter. "Why, Father? Have the nuts gone?"

"A good many of them have," said Father. "Well, you may go. Remember never to take anything without asking, won't you?"

"Oh, yes, Daddy," said all the children, and off they went. But they were very worried, because they couldn't bear to think that their father should even dream that they could take the nuts without asking him first.

"Whoever can it be?" said Peter. "The baby-sitter hates nuts, so it can't be her."

"And the cleaning lady's been away ill for a month, so it can't be her!" said George.

"Well, that only leaves us three and Mummy and Daddy!" said Susan, puzzled. "Who on earth can it be?"

"We'll just wait and see if any more go," said Peter. "Then, if they do, we'll have to do something about it!"

The next week, Father went up to the attic again, to look at the nuts – and dear me, a whole lot more had vanished! How puzzled and grieved he was! He felt certain that it must be one of the children.

But each of them said, "No, Daddy," when he asked them.

"Well, it must be one of you," said

Father, sadly. "It can't be anyone else. It grieves me very much, children, for I didn't think any of you would do such a stupid thing."

Susan went out of the room crying, for she loved her father. George and Peter went very red, and when they were in the playroom they put their arms round Susan and hugged her and told her not to mind.

"It's not us, we know that," said George. "But it looks as if it quite easily might be us, so we can't blame Daddy for asking. The thing to do is to show him that it isn't us. Let's ask him to lock the door."

So they went to ask Father. "Very well," he said, and he locked the door and put the key in his pocket.

But still the nuts vanished! Father became more puzzled than ever. He simply couldn't make it out.

"Anyway, that proves it isn't us," said George, and Father smiled and said yes, it did, and he was very pleased indeed.

"I think it must be the fairies," said Susan. "Daddy, will you let us hide in the attic cupboard and watch one night?"

"No," said Father, laughing. "If you want to do any watching, you must do it in the daytime."

"But the fairies wouldn't come then," said Susan. But Father wouldn't agree to night-time watching, so Susan decided to watch in the daytime.

That afternoon the three children climbed the stairs to the attic, feeling rather excited. They were quite determined to catch the thief.

They went to the cupboard and settled themselves behind the curtains. For a long time nothing happened. Susan began to feel sleepy – but suddenly George poked her in the back.

"Shh! Shh!" he said. "Do you hear something?"

Susan and Peter listened. Yes! There was a little scraping noise that was coming from somewhere. Then there was a bump and a slither, and a patter across the floor!

Was it the fairies? How the children's hearts beat! They peeped through the curtains, and watched the box of nuts. And then they saw the thief!

Who do you think it was? Why, it was a little squirrel who lived in the

pinewoods nearby! The pretty creature
had climbed up a tree by the attic
window, jumped to the top of the open
window, leaped down, and come to the
store of nuts every day!

"Oh!" said Susan. "So that's the thief!
The cheeky little fellow!"

The squirrel heard the children in the
cupboard, and pricked up his ears.
Suddenly George rushed out from behind
the curtains and shut the window with a
bang. The door was already shut, so the
squirrel was fairly caught!

"Let's fetch Daddy!" said Susan. "Then
he'll see who the thief is!"

So George opened the door a little way,
and shouted "Daddy! Mummy! Do come
up to the attic! We've caught the thief!"

The children's parents came running
up and slipped in through the door.

"There!" said Susan, pointing to the
squirrel. "What do you think of our thief,
Daddy?"

"Well, well, well!" said Father, in
astonishment. "A squirrel! Whoever
would have thought it! He must have

discovered our nuts and thought what a fine treasure-store he had found! Open the window and let him go, Peter."

When the window was opened the squirrel hopped out and disappeared down the tree.

"The mystery is solved," said Mother, "and a good thing too! Come along downstairs, children, and I will give you cherry cake for tea as a reward for your discovery!"

"Hurrah!" shouted the children, and off they rushed downstairs!

The Most
Peculiar Knocker

In Hurry-Up Village there lived some naughty goblin children called Tuffy, Smick and Woff. The tricks they got up to!

They would lean over the walls of people's back gardens and snip their clothes-lines so that the clothes would tumble right down into the mud.

They would all climb up to the little bedroom that Tuffy had at the top of his house, and pour water down on passers-by. And then they would go up to people's front doors and knock loudly and run away.

So you can see that they were really a perfect nuisance. "There go Tuffy, Smick and Woff," the people would say, seeing the three children going down the street.

119

"I wonder what mischief they're up to now?"

One day Mr Candleshoe came to live in the cottage at the end of the street. He was a funny old fellow, who always sang little songs to himself whenever he went out. Tuffy and the others thought it would be fine fun to tease him.

"He's got a wonderful new knocker on his door," said Tuffy. "It's a really strange one – just like a man's hand! I guess it must have been a magic one at some time or other."

It certainly was a peculiar knocker. It knocked extremely loudly, too, but that was a good thing because Mr Candleshoe was rather deaf, and he wouldn't have heard if anyone had knocked softly.

Ratta-tatta-TAT! said the knocker, loudly, when the postman called.

Ratta-TATTA-TAT! it said, even more loudly, when Mr Candleshoe's friend Mr Sharp-Eye, called. Mr Sharp-Eye was a wizard, it was said. He knew a lot of spells, and Tuffy, Woff and Smick kept out of his way. They didn't like the way

he looked at them when they met him!

"I feel he might turn me into a black beetle or something," said Smick, "and I don't like it."

Now, Tuffy soon found that it was fun to bang Mr Candleshoe's knocker. The first time he did it, he had to deliver a parcel there. He crashed the knocker up and down.

RATTA-TATTA-RATTA-TATTA! The noise almost made Mr Candleshoe jump out of his skin.

"Jumping pigs and piglets!" he cried. "What's that?"

He hurried to the door, falling over the mat on the way. Tuffy thought it really was one of the funniest things he had ever seen.

"Now don't you crash on my door like that again," said Mr Candleshoe, when he saw Tuffy. "I won't have it! You're a bad goblin. I shan't give you any money for bringing the parcel."

"Ho!" thought Tuffy, going down the steps. "Oho! So he won't give me any money, the mean old miser! Well I'll soon make him wish he had!"

He went to find Smick and Woff. He told them how he had crashed the knocker on Mr Candleshoe's door and made the old man jump. "He's a mean fellow," said Tuffy. "We'll go and do a lot more crashing, shall we?"

So Smick used to go and knock loudly on his way to school in the morning, and Woff used to do it whenever he passed, which was quite often.

Ratta-tatta-TAT! RATTA-TAT! You should have heard that knocker going – morning, afternoon and evening! Mr

Candleshoe would jump out of his chair and tear to the door – and nobody would be there!

He was puzzled at first. He thought whoever was there must be invisible. But they weren't, of course. They had just run away.

Then Mr Candleshoe gave up going to the door to open it. But the very times he didn't go, it would be the postman with a parcel, or Mrs Lucy coming along with a dish of hot cakes, or the milkman asking if he wanted any cream left that day.

"What am I to do, what am I to do?" said poor old Mr Candleshoe to his friend,

Mr Sharp-Eye. "That knocker makes me jump from morning to night – and when I answer the door, there's nobody there – and if I don't answer it there's sure to be somebody!"

"You want a little magic rubbed into the knocker!" said Mr Sharp-Eye, with a grin. "That's what you want, my good friend. I'll put some there for you. Let's see – your knocker is in the shape of a big hand, isn't it? I'll just go and rub a little of my yellow ointment into it. You'll soon find out who comes and bangs on it, Mr Candleshoe. And your knocker will hold him tight for you!"

Mr Sharp-Eye rubbed in the magic ointment. Then he said goodbye to Mr

Candleshoe and went home.

It wasn't long before Tuffy was along that way again. He looked up the street and down. Nobody about. Now for a good old crash with that knocker! He'd make Mr Candleshoe fall out of his chair with fright!

But it so happened that Mr Candleshoe had gone out just after his friend had walked home and there was nobody in his cottage! So when Tuffy rapped on the knocker, *RATTA-TATTA-TAT*, there was no one indoors to hear it.

Tuffy had tight hold of the knocker as he knocked – but something strange happened before he had finished. The brass knocker, which was shaped like a hand, suddenly took hold of him! Yes, it twisted round, and held Tuffy's hand so tightly that he squealed!

"Oooh! What's happening? Ooh! Let go, let go! Ooooh!"

Tuffy couldn't take his hand away! The knocker had got it far too tightly. He pulled and he tugged, but it wasn't a bit of good. He couldn't get away.

Then he guessed what had happened. Mr Candleshoe had some magic in his knocker, and the knocker was busy using it! It would hold Tuffy there till Mr Candleshoe came back – and then what would happen?

Tuffy began to squeal. His two friends Smick and Woff came by and they stopped when they heard Tuffy's yells. "What's the matter?" they shouted in surprise.

"Come and pull, come and pull!" cried Tuffy. "This knocker's got hold of me!"

So Smick and Woff went to pull and, dear me, they pulled so hard that the knocker came right off the door! Then Tuffy raced home as fast as he could, afraid that Mr Candleshoe might come back and catch him if he stayed a moment longer.

The knocker still had hold of his hand! Tuffy couldn't get rid of it. It held tightly on to his fingers, and it wouldn't let them go at all!

Tuffy put it into ice-cold water. No good. Then he put it into very hot water

and almost scalded the skin off his own hand. No good at all! The knocker held him as tightly as ever.

Then Tuffy knew that nothing would ever make the magic knocker let go of his hand, unless Mr Candleshoe helped, and he began to howl.

In came his father and mother, alarmed. When they saw Tuffy and the knocker, they were even more astonished.

"Get it off, oh please get it off!" wept Tuffy.

"It's a knocker!" said his father. "And it looks like Candleshoe's too. Tuffy, how did you come to get it like this?"

Tuffy wailed out his story. His father listened sternly. "Ah – at last you have found someone who can punish you for playing your silly, annoying tricks!" he said. "Well, Tuffy, either you will have to live with that knocker, or you will have to go to Mr Candleshoe and confess to him what has happened!"

"I'm afraid to do that, I'm afraid!" howled Tuffy.

But he had to go in the end, because,

you see, he couldn't write, or wash his hand properly, or even undress, with the knocker holding him by the hand like that!

"Ha!" said Mr Candleshoe, when Tuffy stood before him, his face red with crying. "So it was you trying to be funny, bringing me to the door a dozen times a day! Well, I think that you've got a fine punishment!"

"Please take the knocker off my hand!" wept Tuffy. "Please take it off."

"I've got a new knocker now," said Mr Candleshoe. "I don't need that one. You can have it."

"I don't *wannnt* it!" wailed Tuffy. "Oh, take it off, Mr Candleshoe, and I'll never never be bad again."

"Well – I'll take it off," said Mr Candleshoe, "but I don't want it back. It can live with you, Tuffy. But I warn you – if you get up to any tricks, the knocker will chase you and try to take hold of your hand once more!"

And goodness me, it does! His father never needs to punish Tuffy now. Whenever he's naughty, the knocker jumps up from its corner, and chases him round the room. What a fine time that knocker has and no mistake! I'm sure Tuffy's sorry now that he ever played the silly game of knocking at doors and running away.

The Pedlar's Needle

Flip and Binkle Bunny were at breakfast when Pedlar Polecat knocked at their door.

"All sorts of things for sale!" he said. "Cloth for coats, cloth for trousers, buttons of all colours, and needles to sew them on with!"

"Let's see them!" said Binkle. "We're going to a party tomorrow, and we'd rather like a new suit each. My! What pretty colours they are!"

"Let's buy some," said Flip. "We've got some money."

So they bought some striped material for coats, and some checked cloth for trousers. They bought some buttons and some needles, and gave Pedlar Polecat the money.

"Thank you!" he said. "Now, would you like to see something very rare?"

"Yes!" said Flip and Binkle both together.

The pedlar opened a tiny box and showed them a little red needle.

"It's a magic needle," he said. "It was given to me by Witch Weasel in return for a bit of help I once gave her."

"What's magic about it?" asked Binkle.

"I'll tell you," said the pedlar. "If ever I get a hole in my sock, I just say 'Sew, needle, sew,' in a loud voice, and it mends it all by itself!"

"Goodness!" said Flip. "What a wonderful thing, to be sure!"

"Now I must be going," said Pedlar Polecat, and packed up his bag. "Goodbye!" he called, and went on his way.

Binkle and Flip carried their goods indoors.

"We'll have to hurry up and make our suits, if we're going to wear them tomorrow," said Flip.

"What a bother," yawned Binkle. "I did so want to go fishing today. Can't

you make them both, Flip?"

"No, I can't!" cried Flip, indignantly. "Here, help me clear the breakfast table, Binkle, and we'll start."

Binkle took the tablecloth to the door and shook it. He noticed something lying on the step, and bent to pick it up. Then he stared at it in surprise.

"Flip!" he called, "do come and look. Pedlar Polecat's dropped his magic needle, and it's on our doorstep!"

"You'd better run after him with it," said Flip.

"All right," answered Binkle. Then he stopped and thought.

"Flip!" he said, in an excited voice. "Let's borrow it for a bit, and get it to make our new clothes for us. Then we can go out fishing!"

"All right," agreed Flip. So the two bunnies put their new checked and striped cloth on a stool, and placed the needle on top of it.

"Sew, needle, sew!" commanded Binkle.

At once the needle began to fly in and out of the cloth, as quickly as could be. Flip and Binkle could see no cotton, but that didn't seem to matter.

"Look! It's finished a coat," Flip said excitedly, "and now it's beginning on the trousers!"

The bunnies watched until the needle had finished its work, and once more lay still on top of the two nice new suits.

"Now we'll go off for our day's fishing!" chuckled Binkle. He and Flip took their rods and lines and started out. They fished all day without having a single bite, and at last started home again.

Flip looked rather gloomy.

"Cheer up, Flip!" said Binkle, laughing. "Think of going to the party tomorrow in two fine new suits that we haven't had to make ourselves!"

They arrived home and put on the kettle for tea. Then they went to try on their new suits.

But oh, what do you think? There were no new suits there! Only a neat pile of checked and striped cloth and buttons. The magic needle was gone.

"What happened?" cried the bunnies. Then Flip saw a note on the table. It was from Pedlar Polecat. He read it out loud:

"I came back to look for my needle," it said, "and found you had used it instead of running after me to give it back. I'm afraid your new suits will have all the magic taken out of them when I have gone away with my needle! P.P."

"That just punishes us!" sobbed Flip. "I knew we should have taken it back! Now we must sit up all night and make our suits ourselves!"

And so they did, and when they went to the party, who should be there but Pedlar Polecat! You can just guess how he chuckled when he saw the two bad bunnies!

It's Nice to
Have a Friend

Tibs was a farm cat. She was a little tabby, with fine big whiskers and a nice long tail.

Punch was the farm dog. He was a big collie with a bushy tail and a very loud bark. He didn't like cats one little bit and Tibs didn't like dogs.

Tibs hardly ever went near Punch unless he was tied up, because she knew he would chase her, and Punch was always on the watch for her so that he could tear after her and send her flying up to the top of the wall, hissing and spitting. Then he would bark the place down!

Now, one day when Punch was tied up he came out into the yard on his long chain to sniff at a roller that somebody had left there. He walked round it – and somehow or other his chain got twisted, and he couldn't get back to his kennel. There he was, held tightly by the roller, his chain pulling at his neck.

Punch pulled at it. He rolled over to try and get it loose – and all that happened was that he twisted his chain so much that it almost choked him!

He couldn't bark, he could only make a whine or a growl. So nobody heard him and nobody came to help him. He choked and struggled, but his chain was too tightly twisted round the heavy roller for him to get free.

Only Tibs, the farm cat, heard the noises he was making. She jumped on to the top of the wall and looked at poor Punch. What peculiar noises! What was the matter with him?

"Tibs!" croaked Punch. "Help me. I'm choking."

Tibs jumped down and had a look. No – she couldn't help him. She didn't know anything about chains! But she was sorry for Punch, and she thought of something else. She ran to the farmhouse and mewed loudly.

Mrs Straws, the farmer's wife, came to the door. "What is it?" she said. Tibs ran a little way away and looked back. The farmer's wife followed her – and then she, too, heard the strange noises that Punch was making out in the yard.

She went to see what they were – and in a minute or two she had undone the chain, untwisted it, patted poor Punch, and given him a long drink of water!

Punch looked at Tibs on the wall. "Thank you," he said. "You can come down and sit near me. I shall never chase you again. You saved me from choking."

But Tibs didn't really trust him. She would never come down from the wall. Still, they had many a talk together and that was nice for both of them.

Then one day Tibs didn't come. She didn't come for three days, and then she told Punch why.

"I've got four little kittens," she told him proudly. "They're my very own. They're in the kitchen. But I do wish the children would leave them alone. They are always pulling them about, and it worries me."

The next day Tibs looked even more worried. "Bobby took one of my kittens and dropped it," she said. "I'm going to take them away from the kitchen. I shall put them in the barn."

So she took each of her kittens by the neck and carried them one by one to a corner of the barn. But the children found them there and took them back

to the kitchen again. They were like live toys to them, and they wanted to play with them!

Tibs was unhappy. She liked the children and she didn't want to scratch them. "But what am I to do, Punch?" she said. "One of my kittens has a bad leg because Bobby squeezed it too hard yesterday. I wish I could think of somewhere else to take them."

Punch listened, his big head on one side. "I know a place where nobody would ever find them," he said. "But I don't think you'd like it. It's a place where nobody would ever, ever look."

"Where?" asked Tibs.

"Here in my kennel!" said Punch. "There's plenty of good warm straw – and plenty of room for you and your kittens at the back. I promise not to sit on you. I'll be very, very careful. You were good to me once – now let me be kind to you!"

Tibs thought about it. Did she trust Punch or didn't she? He was a dog. She was a cat. She didn't know if they could really be friends. Still – she would try!

So, when nobody was about, Tibs carried each of her kittens by its neck, all the way from the kitchen to the yard where the kennel was. One by one she laid the little things in the warm straw at the back. Then she settled down on them herself, purring happily.

Punch was very good. He didn't even let his tail rest on the kittens, and he gave them all the room he could. He even licked them when Tibs wasn't there, and when one of them patted his nose he was surprised and delighted.

The children looked all over the place for the kittens. They called and called Tibs. But she didn't come. She wasn't going to give her hiding-place away! Her kittens were safe and happy now. Punch sat in his kennel, so that nobody could even peep in. Aha! Look where you like, Bobby and Betty, you won't find the kittens!

"It's nice to have a friend," purred Tibs. "Nobody knows where I am. Keep my secret, Punch."

He will, of course – and we certainly won't tell Bobby and Betty, will we?

Games in Goblinland

Allan loved playing games indoors on a rainy day. He had draughts, snap and beat-your-neighbour-out-of-doors. I expect you know how to play them all, don't you?

But nobody liked playing games with Allan because he always wanted to win – and if he didn't, he either cheated or flew into a temper and wouldn't play any more!

His father was angry with him. "You must learn to lose, as well as to win!" he often said to Allan. "You must never cheat, and as for flying into a temper and throwing the cards and the counters about – well! You ought to be ashamed of yourself!"

Now one day it was wet, and a friend of

Allan's mother came to ask if Allan would like to bring his games to her house and play them with Michael, her little boy. So Allan took a basket with his draught board and draughtsmen in, and his two packs of cards to play snap and beat-your-neighbour-out-of- doors.

He ran down a little path that went down the side of a field and, as he ran, the box of draughtsmen upset and rolled out of the basket. Allan bent down to pick them up. He found all but one, and this last one he could not find!

He thought it must have gone into the thick hedge that grew by the side of the path, so he crawled into it – and then he had the surprise of his life!

In the shelter of the hedge sat three small goblins, playing a curious game with fans and balls that Allan had never seen before. He stared and stared – and they stared back.

"Come and play," said one of the goblins. He offered Allan a fan and two balls. The little boy took them in delight and sat down beside the goblins. This was an exciting adventure!

But he couldn't play the game, however much he tried – so he fetched his basket and games, and showed them to the goblins.

"We do not know how to play those games," they said.

"Oh, they are easy," said Allan, at once, delighted to think that if the goblins did not know how to play the games, he would easily win! "This game is called draughts. And this one is called snap. And this one, played with these cards,

is called beat-your-neighbour-out-of-doors!"

He showed the goblins how to play draughts – and one of them began to play with him. But, you know, goblin brains are sharp – and the little fellow easily beat Allan! The little boy lost his temper – and what do you suppose he did? He picked up the draughtboard and threw it hard at the surprised goblin!

There was a silence for a moment. Then the goblin stood up and frowned angrily.

"So that's how you play your game of draughts!" he said. "I suppose you play your games of snap and beat-your-neighbour-out-of- doors in the same way! Well! Come with us and we will show you how we play those games in our country! We will see if you like that!"

The three goblins caught hold of the bad-tempered little boy and pushed him through the hedge to the other side – and to Allan's enormous astonishment he saw that he was in a small town of little hillocks, in each of which lived a goblin. The three goblins with Allan clapped their hands and called out something. At once the doors in the hillock-houses flew open and out came scores of small goblins just like the others, all dressed in grey suits and hats, and all with pointed ears and feet.

"We want to teach this boy a few games," said one of the three goblins, with a grin. "It seems to us that he doesn't know how to play the games he has with him. First we would like to teach him how to play draughts!"

"Ho, ho, ho!" laughed all the goblins at once. "We shall show him!" They stood in a ring and took hands. "Come into the middle!" they shouted to Allan. "We will show you how to play our game of draughts!"

Allan was pushed into the middle of the ring. Then the goblins danced round once, and sang a strange, chanting song that went like this:

"North wind blow!
South wind too!
East and West wind
Where are you?"

Immediately there came the four

winds, blowing hard from the north, south, east and west. They came right into the ring of dancing goblins, and began to blow poor Allan!

His cap flew off, and his coat flew open. His hair stood up and there was a loud whistling in his ears. He could hardly stand upright, and he felt dreadfully cold.

"This is our game of draughts!" shouted the goblins in glee. "Isn't it draughty? Do you feel a draught? Do you think you will win? It's no use losing your temper in this game – because the winds won't let you! They do love a game of draughts!"

Allan became so out of breath with the blowing of the four winds that he could not say a single word. He staggered about in the ring of goblins, puffing and blowing, trying to keep his coat on and feeling colder and colder!

As suddenly as they had come, the winds went. The goblins unlinked their hands and laughed at Allan, who sat down to get his breath. He felt giddy.

"Did you like our game of draughts?" asked the goblins. "Wasn't it fun? Now we'll show you how to play snap!"

They made a ring again, and put Allan in the middle. Then they began to chant another song:

"Here's a chap
Who likes to snap.
Play with him, pup,
And snap him up!"

Then into the ring there ran a big puppydog, full of fun and nonsense. When he saw Allan he ran at him and snapped playfully at the little boy's legs.

151

"Don't, don't!" shouted Allan. "Go away! I don't want to play with you, you nasty little puppy. Go away!"

He flapped his handkerchief at the puppy, and it woofed joyfully. It snapped at the handkerchief and tore it in half. Allan became very angry.

"Look what you've done!" he cried. "You've spoilt my handkerchief. Go away!"

The goblins shrieked with laughter to see the puppy playing snap with Allan. The little boy took his cap and tried to smack the puppy with it. But the little dog snapped at it eagerly, snatched it right out of Allan's hand and ran off round the ring with it!

"He's snapped the cap, he's snapped the cap!" yelled the goblins. "Oh, doesn't he play snap well? Do you like the way we play snap here, Allan?"

The puppy shook the cap and bit it hard. Then he ran at Allan again and began to snap at his coat. The small boy was almost in tears, for, although he could see that the puppy would not hurt

him, he was very angry to have to play such a strange, silly game of snap!

The puppy jumped up and snapped a button off Allan's coat. The goblins cheered him and then sent him out of the ring. Allan picked up his torn handkerchief and his bitten cap and button.

"Well, the puppy won that game!" said the goblins. "Now for a game of beat-your-neighbour-out-of- doors!"

They took Allan to a small hillock-house and pushed him inside. They shut the door. He was left alone for a minute or two, and then the door suddenly burst open. In came a small goblin pretending to be very angry. He waved a stick at Allan and shouted, "Get out of my house or I will beat you out!" Allan rushed out at once and the goblin chased after him. Seeing the next house with the door standing open, Allan rushed inside and banged the door. But, dear me, there was a goblin in there, and he had a stick too! He jumped up and shouted:

"Get out of my house or I will beat you out!" Allan gave a shout and rushed out again, with the goblin after him, waving his stick. In and out of the hillock-houses they rushed, and at last Allan ran into an open door again, for he could see there was no goblin inside. He banged the door and bolted it. Then he sat down to get his breath.

"They can't get me out of here!" he thought to himself. But he was mistaken – for there came a rumbling in the chimney – and down came a goblin, almost dropping on top of Allan, who had bent down to see what the noise was.

"Get out of my house or I will beat you out!" shouted the goblin gleefully, waving his stick. Allan unbolted the door in a hurry and rushed outside.

All the other goblins stood there, grinning and shouting in great delight.

"Do you like the way we play beat-your-neighbour-out-of-doors?" they cried. "Shall we teach you another game? We have a fine one called put-me-in-a-coal-hole!"

Allan thought that didn't sound at all a nice game, so he shook his head.

"No, thank you," he said. "Please let me go to my friend's. He is expecting me. I am sorry I lost my temper when I played draughts with you in the hedge. I like my way of playing our games best. I don't like yours at all."

"Well, if you had played your game properly without losing your temper, we wouldn't have shown you how we could play!" said one of the goblins. "You can go on your way. We don't expect to ever see you here again – unless you forget how to play properly, and want to come and be taught by us!"

"No, I don't, thank you," said Allan. "Goodbye."

Allan went to the thick hedge that grew behind the little town of hillock-houses, and squeezed his way through it. And on the other side was the field he knew so well – and his basket of games lying on the path!

Allan picked up the basket and set off to Michael's house. He was soon there, and Michael opened the door for him. "What a long time you have been!" he said. "Whatever have you been doing? Did you get lost?"

"No – not exactly lost," said Allan, and he wouldn't say any more, for he was too ashamed to tell Michael all that had happened to him.

"Come along to the playroom and we will play our games there," said Michael. "We'll play draughts first." So up they went, and set out the board on the playroom table. They put out the counters and began the game.

Michael was cleverer than Allan at the game, and soon took all his men – but do

you suppose Allan cheated or lost his
temper? No – not a bit of it! He said,
"You've won, Michael. Now let's play
snap."

So they got out the snap cards, and
soon they were snapping away, taking
each other's pile of cards. Allan thought
of the way the goblins played snap with
the puppy dog, and he couldn't help
thinking that his and Michael's way was
very much nicer!

"Snap!" said Michael suddenly, while
Allan was thinking about the goblins and
forgetting to look at the cards.

Oh! Michael had snapped all his pile of
cards – and had won!

"It isn't fair," said Allan, "because I
was just thinking about..."

And just as he spoke he thought he
heard a little sound of goblin chuckling
away to himself. He looked round quickly.
No – there wasn't a goblin to be seen.

"It's all right," said Allan. "It's quite
fair. I should have been looking at the
game."

Then they began to play beat-your-

neighbour-out-of-doors, and would you believe it, Michael seemed to have all the kings, queens and aces in the pack – so it wasn't very long before he had beaten Allan again. But this time the little boy was not going to say a word about the win not being fair – nor was he going to lose his temper!

"It's your game again!" he said to Michael. "Jolly good!"

And he thought he heard a whisper somewhere: "Jolly good, Allan! Well done!" But though he looked all round again, there was nobody there at all.

Allan plays games as they should be played now – no cheating, no grumbling, no losing of tempers. And one day he is going to squeeze through that thick hedge and tell those goblins something. He wants to say, "Thank you for teaching me all you did! I'll never forget it." Won't they be surprised?

Billy's Shopping

"Billy, darling," said Mother one fine morning, "will you walk down to the village and go to the shops for me? I want a nice brown loaf from the baker's, some tea from the grocer's, and a pound of sausages from the butcher's."

"Of course I'll go to the shops for you, Mum!" said Billy, and he put down his book and jumped up. He took the basket from its place in the corner and went to the door.

"You are a good little boy, Billy," said Mother. "Here is some money for yourself. Buy some sweets or a comic."

"Oh, thank you, Mum!" said Billy, and off he went. He went to the baker's first where he bought a large brown loaf. Then he went to the grocer's and asked for a packet of tea. Lastly, he went to the butcher's and waited in the queue for a pound of sausages. They all went nicely into his basket.

"Now I have my money to spend," thought Billy. He ran along to the sweet-shop – but on the way he came to the greengrocer's. Oh, what a lovely lot of apples, pears and plums he could see in the window! There they all lay, red, yellow and purple, and Billy stood and looked at them in delight.

Billy remembered that his mother loved to eat apples. He could buy her one – a nice, rosy, red one! Then he remembered his little sister Nell. Perhaps he could buy her a plum too. That would be a good way to spend his money. How surprised Mum and Nell would be when he came home and gave them the fruit!

"Yes, that's it," he said to himself, "I will buy a ripe red apple for Mum and a juicy plum for Nell!"

He went into the shop.

"Please may I have an apple and a plum?" he asked the shopkeeper. He put

his money down on the counter. The
shopkeeper put a big rosy apple and a
ripe purple plum into a paper bag and
gave them to Billy. He popped them both
into his basket, and galloped home like a
horse!

"I've bought an apple for you, Mum,
and a plum for Nell!" he said when he
had arrived back at his house. How
surprised and pleased they were!

"I really do think you are the kindest
little boy in the world, Billy!" said
Mother, and she kissed him.

"Give Billy one of the new chocolate cakes you have made this morning, Mummy," said Nell. "He has spent his own money on us, and has bought us some lovely fruit – so we really must give him something too!"

"Oooh! I do love chocolate cakes!" said Billy. Then down they all sat. Mother ate her apple and she said it was very sweet. Nell ate her plum and she said it was very juicy. Billy ate his cake and he said it was by far the nicest chocolate cake he had ever tasted!

So they were all very happy indeed!

The Beautiful
Big Bone

Once upon a time Bundle the spaniel had a beautiful big bone. It had two nobbly ends and a long, thick middle, and it smelled lovely.

Bundle was very proud of his bone. He didn't show it to Cosy the cat because he was afraid she might gnaw one of the ends off. Bundle spent an awfully long time gnawing on the bone, and when he was tired of it he hid it, so that when he wanted another chew at it he would know where to find it.

"I'll hide it in the cabbage bed," Bundle thought. "No one goes there now. I think it will be a very good place."

So he dug away the earth and hid it there. Cosy saw him and wondered what he could be doing. The next day Bundle dug up his bone again and had another good chew at it. Then he carried it off in his mouth to bury it once more.

"Are you going to put that in the cabbage bed again?" asked Cosy, meeting him round the corner. Bundle growled at her.

"You mind your own business!" he said.

Bundle trotted off, thinking hard. What a nuisance! Now Cosy knew exactly where he had decided to hide his bone.

"Never mind!" thought Bundle. "I'll hide it somewhere else – somewhere that Cosy will never guess! I'll hide it in the rubbish heap!"

So he went to the rubbish heap at the bottom of the garden and dug in the rubbish there to hide his bone. Cosy watched him from under a bush.

"I suppose Bundle doesn't want his bone any more, as he's putting it on the rubbish heap," thought Cosy. "Well, I'll have a lick at it when he's gone."

So, when Bundle had gone indoors to snooze by the fire, Cosy scampered over to the rubbish heap. She soon found the beautiful big bone and she dragged it out. She took it into a quiet corner where she began to lick it.

Her tongue was very rough and she managed to scrape off a few bits of meat. Then she decided it would be lovely to gnaw the bone, but her teeth were simply not strong enough.

"Woof!" said a voice in her ear suddenly, and made her jump high into the air. "Lend me that bone, Cosy!"

It was Shadow, the big sheepdog from the farm. He was a gentle fellow, and Cosy was not afraid of him.

"All right," she said. "You can have it, because I'm sure Bundle doesn't want it any more. He put it on the rubbish heap."

"What a stupid dog!" said Shadow, and picked up the bone to carry it away. He took it to the farmyard, went into his kennel with it, and lay there, licking and gnawing very happily.

Now, when Bundle went to the rubbish heap, to his great surprise he found no bone there. He sat down and wailed miserably. It wasn't long before Cosy heard him.

"Whatever can the matter be?" she said.

"My beautiful bone's gone!" cried Bundle, and he wailed again.

"It's all right. Shadow has got it," said Cosy, and was just going to explain that she had lent it to him when Bundle tore off down the garden, out of the gate and into the lane that led to the farm, before

Cosy could say another word to him.

Bundle arrived at the farm. He saw Shadow gnawing his beautiful big bone. He went as near as he dared and spoke to Shadow.

"Give me that bone. It's mine."

"Ask for it politely," said Shadow, giving a crunch that sounded very loud to Bundle.

"Don't bite it in half, don't!" wailed poor Bundle. "It's my bone! Give it to me at once, Shadow, you bad dog!"

"Not if you talk like that," said Shadow, licking the bone well.

"Well, what do you want for that bone?" said Bundle at last, thinking that if he didn't get the bone quickly, there wouldn't be any to get.

"I wouldn't mind a nice drink of milk," said Shadow. "I feel very thirsty. You get me a jug of milk and I'll give you the bone."

Bundle ran off to Buttercup the cow. "Could you give me some milk?" he said.

Buttercup looked at him and chewed hard. "I might, if you'll go and ask Neddy the donkey, in the next field, if he'll let me have one of his carrots," said Buttercup. "I just feel somehow I'd like to taste a carrot today."

"Oh, tails and whiskers – Neddy's right at the end of the next field!" said poor Bundle. "By the time I get to him and back, and get some milk and take it to Shadow, my bone will have been eaten!"

But he raced across the field, squeezed under the gate and ran to Neddy, who was crunching up a few carrots the farmer's wife had given him.

"Neddy, will you give me a carrot

for Buttercup the cow?" asked Bundle, panting.

"Well, you'll have to give me something in return," said Neddy. "You go and get me a fine thistle plant to eat."

"What! Do you eat thistles?" said Bundle, surprised. "Aren't they very prickly?"

"Yes. They're delicious," said Neddy. "Go and get me some. Do you see Bleater the goat over there on the common? Well,

there are some fine thistles near him. He will show you them."

Off went poor Bundle again, and came to Bleater, who put down his head and danced round and round Bundle as if he was going to butt him.

"No, don't do that, Bleater. I've only come for some thistles," said Bundle. "Tails and whiskers, aren't they prickly! I can't possibly bite them and take them to Neddy. I should make my mouth bleed."

"Well, I'll pick them for you if you like," said Bleater at once. "My mouth is hard. I don't mind anything. But what will you give me if I do?"

"Oh dear, everyone wants something today," said Bundle. "What do you want, Bleater?"

"Well, do you see that hole in the hedge there?" said Bleater. "There's a hen sitting there, on eggs she has laid. I've always wanted to eat an egg, Bundle. You go and get one for me. My rope won't reach to that gap in the hedge."

So Bundle ran off to the gap, and nosed

his way to the hen. She pecked him and he yelped.

"What do you want?" she said.

"An egg for Bleater, please," said Bundle. The hen gave an angry cluck.

"An egg! What next? For nothing, I suppose?"

"Well – what do you want for it?" said Bundle. The hen put her head on one side and thought hard for a moment.

"One of the eggs I'm sitting on is addled," she said. "I don't mind Bleater having that one, and I dare say a goat would rather eat a bad egg than a good one. You go and get me some corn, Bundle, and then I'll give you the egg."

Bundle ran off to the corn bin. He

knew where it was. But sitting beside it was Cosy!

"Get away, Cosy, I want some corn," said Bundle.

"Be quiet, Bundle!" said Cosy. "I'm watching for the mouse that comes to this bin. You'll frighten it away if you bark like that. Besides, you know very well you don't eat corn!"

"I want it for the hen," Bundle said crossly. "Get away, Cosy, and let me open the bin."

"Now, listen to me, Bundle," said Cosy. "Don't bother about corn for the hen. You go off home and look in your dish. I've put something there for you!"

"Yes – a fish-bone you can't swallow, I suppose!" said Bundle. "Now move away, Cosy, and let me get this corn."

"Well – I'll move away if you let me have half your dinner tonight," said Cosy. Bundle groaned. Everybody wanted something.

"All right," he said. "You can share my dinner, but do let me get the corn."

Cosy moved away. Bundle lifted up the

lid and put his nose in. He got a mouthful of corn and ran off to the hen with it.

He scattered it by her and she pecked it up, clucking loudly. "Now you can have the egg," she said. "The one on the outside, just there."

Bundle picked it up in his mouth and ran off to Bleater the goat with the egg. Bleater was delighted. He pulled up a whole thistle for Bundle, and then ate the egg. It smelled horrible to Bundle, but Bleater thought it was delicious.

Bundle dragged the thistle along by its root. It was the only part of it that wasn't too prickly to hold. He came at last to Neddy the donkey.

"Ah," said Neddy, "just in time! I was going to eat my last carrot, but now you can have it in exchange for this fine thistle."

He gave Bundle a carrot, and then began to crunch up the thistle. Bundle thought it was marvellous not to bother about eating sharp prickles like that. He ran off with the carrot.

Buttercup the cow was waiting. Bundle gave her the carrot and she nibbled at it daintily. "I have no teeth in my top jaw, so it's not as easy to eat a carrot as it is to pull grass," she said. "Still, it's very tasty. There is some milk in a small pail for you over there, Bundle. Can you pick up the handle in your mouth and take it along like that?"

Bundle just managed to, though he spilled a little of the milk on the way. Still, there was plenty left in the pail when he reached Shadow the sheepdog,

who was still lying in his kennel.

"Woof!" said Shadow, and drank up the milk at once. "Most delicious! Thank you!"

"Where's my beautiful big bone?" said Bundle, looking round in alarm. "Oh, Shadow – you haven't eaten it, have you?"

"No," said Shadow. "I gave it back to Cosy. She came and fetched it."

"Well!" said Bundle, and tore off to find Cosy, quite determined to chase her all round the garden and back again if she had taken his bone.

"Cosy! How dare you take my bone from Shadow!" wuffed Bundle, out of breath.

"Well, Bundle, you were so upset about it," said Cosy. "So I went and told him it was yours, and he gave it back to me for you. It's in your dish. I put it there myself. I don't know why you wanted to go rushing round the garden getting corn for hens and things like that all the afternoon!"

"Now, look here Cosy!" said Bundle

fiercely. "Shadow said he'd give me back my bone if I gave him some milk from Buttercup the cow. And she said she'd give me milk if I got a carrot from Neddy for her. And he said he'd give me a carrot if I got him a thistle. And Bleater the goat said he'd give me the thistle if I got him a hen's egg to eat. And the hen said she'd give me an egg if I got her some corn. And *you* said you'd let me have the corn if I gave you half my dinner tonight. And all the time I was rushing about getting presents for everybody my big beautiful bone was sitting in my dish waiting for me!"

Cosy began to laugh. Bundle stared crossly at her. Then he looked so fierce she began to feel rather alarmed.

"I'm going to chase you all round the garden and then bite the hairs off the end of your tail!" said Bundle.

"Now, Bundle, listen – while you do that someone may come along and take your bone out of its dish!" said Cosy, edging away. "Do be sensible, and go and get it while it's safe!"

So poor Bundle ran off to get his bone. He lay in a corner and chewed it. Then he began to laugh. Yes, it was funny the way he had rushed all over the place finding things for people, so that he could get back his bone – and all the time it was waiting for him in his dish!

"You can share my dinner with me if you like!" he called out to Cosy. "Why don't we tell Mistress what I've done this afternoon, and let me make it into a story, shall we?"

So he did – and here it is!

Confetti
and Bells

"Pip! Where ever can you be?" called Aunt Twinkle. "Oh, there you are. Listen, I want your help."

"What sort of help?" asked Pip the pixie. "I don't want to sweep or scrub or..."

"No, that's not the kind of help I want this time," said Aunt Twinkle. "Didn't you know that the sailor doll and Tilly, one of the doll's-house dolls, are getting married today?"

"Are they?" said Pip. "Well, I'll go to the wedding then. But what sort of help do you want, Aunt Twinkle?"

"The toys haven't got any confetti to throw over the sailor doll and Tilly," said his aunt. "And they haven't got any bells to ring, either. Can you and Jinky manage to get some in time for the wedding?"

"Yes, of course!" said Pip. "Jinky, come and help. We've got to get confetti and bells for a wedding."

The two pixies ran off. First they went to the bluebell glade, and picked six fine bluebells. They pulled the blue bells from the stalks and threaded them on silver thread. They put a ringing spell inside, and then went back to hang them up for the toys.

"They'll ring at exactly the right moment," said Pip. "Now we're off to get the confetti. We'll be back in a minute!"

They ran to the hawthorn hedge. The may was in full bloom, and its sweet, spicy scent filled the air. Pip looked up at the masses of snow-white blossom.

"Blow, wind, blow for a few minutes!" he cried, and the wind blew. Down fluttered a thousand tiny white petals from the may-hedge, and fell over the ground.

"Pick them up, Jinky," said Pip. The

two picked up all the white petals, popped them into paper bags and ran off to the toys.

"The finest, sweetest-smelling confetti in the world!" said Pip. "Where's the bride? Here she comes!" And he threw handfuls of confetti over her – how pretty the petals looked flying in the air. Then the blue bells began to ring, and everyone cheered.

Who had the biggest slices of the wedding cake? I'll leave you to guess!

Little Rubbalong
Plays a Trick

One day little Rubbalong was mending shoes in his mother's cottage, humming a little song.

> "Tippety-tap,
> My work I begin,
> Tippety-tap,
> And a nail goes in!
> I use good leather
> From heel to toe,
> No matter the weather
> Warm and dry will you go!"

He finished a shoe and threw it on one side. Then he picked up a pair of stout laced boots. "Ma!" he called, "here's a pair of Old Man Borrow's boots. He owes us for the last ones I did – and he

borrowed some money from you, didn't
he? Shall I mend this pair?"

Ma Rubbalong came over to look at
them. She gave a little smile that meant
mischief.

"Now you listen to me, Rubbalong,"
she said. "Old Man Borrow ought to have
a lesson about borrowing and never
paying back. I think we'll give it to him!"

"How, Ma?" asked Rubbalong, as he
began to mend the boots.

"Well, Old Man Borrow is vain," said
Ma. "We will give him that pair of yellow

leather laces for his boots. He'll be so proud of them. But I'll rub a go-tight spell on them."

"How will that work, Ma?" asked Rubbalong, beginning to smile.

"Whenever he meets anyone that he owes money to, or has borrowed things from without returning them, those laces will pull themselves so tight he'll hardly be able to walk!" said Ma. "And what is more, Rubbalong, we'll tell everyone about the spell! Old Man Borrow will be very surprised when he finds himself meeting so many people that he owes money to!"

Rubbalong laughed. "What a joke! You're an absolute wonder at fitting the right spell to the right people, Ma!"

He mended the boots. Then he took the lovely yellow laces that Ma Rubbalong had rubbed with her go-tight spell, and he threaded them deftly through the holes. "There! And now here comes Old Man Borrow for his boots!" said Rubbalong. "I wonder if he'll pay me."

He didn't, of course. "I'll look in tomorrow with the money," he said. "I'm in a bit of a hurry today." And off he went with a boot under each arm.

Well, Rubbalong soon spread the news about that there was a spell on Old Man Borrow's boots. "If you see him wearing yellow laces go and meet him," said Rubbalong. "They'll pull themselves so tight that he'll hardly be able to walk! He won't pay you what he owes you then – but maybe those laces will make him pay up in the end!"

Well, all kinds of people set out to meet Old Man Borrow the first day he wore his mended boots, very proud indeed of the yellow laces in them. Mr Tuck-In was the first. He had lent Old Man Borrow five pounds and wanted it back. Old Man Borrow tried to slip down a side turning but Mr Tuck-In marched right up to him.

And those yellow laces pulled themselves tight. Tighter still. And then so tight that they almost cut into Old Man Borrow's legs. He looked down in fright.

He could hardly walk. He had to hobble beside Mr Tuck-In for quite a

long way, promising to pay back the five pounds as soon as he could. He couldn't even run away!

The laces loosened as soon as Mr Tuck-In went. Old Man Borrow heaved a sigh of relief. How strange! What had happened? Had his legs suddenly swollen up and got too large for his boots? He bent down and loosened the laces a little.

Then he met Dame Scarey. She hurried towards him to ask him to return the ladder she had lent him. And goodness gracious, those laces tightened themselves again, and Old Man Borrow groaned in fright. He began to hobble, and Dame Scarey smiled to herself as she saw Ma Rubbalong's spell working. She spoke to him sternly about her ladder and then left him. The laces became loose again. Old Man Borrow just couldn't understand it!

The people he met that morning! And dear me, every one of them had lent Old Man Borrow something and spoke about it crossly. He began to feel most annoyed.

"There must be something wrong with

these boots," he said at last. "I'll go and complain to Rubbalong."

So off he went and complained loudly and bitterly. "It's not the boots," said Rubbalong. "It's the laces. There must be some spell on them. You'd better give me them back."

"Oh no," said Old Man Borrow, hastily. "I like them. Besides, you gave me them for nothing. They're very fine."

"All right. Keep them then," said Rubbalong. "But let's find out if they have a spell on them or not. You say your boots felt very tight when you met Mr Tuck-In – you owe him five pounds, don't you? And Dame Scarey? You've still got her ladder, haven't you? And Mrs Well-I-Never – and Old Father Whiskers, and … well, dear me, how strange, Old Man Borrow! You owe something to all of these people!"

"What difference does that make to my boots?" said Old Man Borrow, sulkily.

"Well, let's just see," said Rubbalong. "Do your boots feel tight now? Oh, they do – you say the laces are cutting into

He'd just have to put up with the spell, if that was what it was!

He couldn't stand it for long, though – the laces could make themselves tighter still, and they did. And now Mr Tuck-In has got back his five pounds, and Dame Scarey has got her ladder, and everyone else is getting their things back too.

Ma Rubbalong did laugh.

"Let's hope the spell will last a nice long time," she said. "By that time we will all be calling Old Man Borrow by a quite different name."

"Yes. Old Man Pay-Back!" said little Rubbalong. "And it will all be because of your yellow laces, Ma!"

your legs. Well, you owe me money, Old Man Borrow. Pay up, and see if the boots feel all right again. If they do, we'll know it has to be those laces!"

Old Man Borrow scowled, but he paid up.

And hey presto! The laces loosened, and the boots no longer felt tight!

"There you are," said Rubbalong. "Just what I told you. Better give me those laces back, Old Man Borrow."

But the mean old fellow wasn't going to give back something he had got for nothing. He scowled again and went off.